Cultural St

Theorizing Politic

VOLUME 12 NUMBE 1998

Special issue:
Un/fixing Representations

Edited by
Judith Farquhar
Tomoko Masuzawa
and
Carol Mavor

Editorial Statement

Cultural Studies continues to expand and flourish, in large part because the field keeps changing. Cultural studies scholars are addressing new questions and discourses, continuing to debate long-standing issues, and reinventing critical traditions. More and more universities have some formal cultural studies presence; the number of books and journals in the field is rapidly increasing. *Cultural Studies* welcomes these developments. We understand the expansion, reflexivity and internal critique of cultural studies to be both signs of its vitality and signature components of its status as a field. At the same time, cultural studies has been – and will no doubt continue to be – the subject of numerous attacks, launched from various perspectives and sites. These have to be taken seriously and answered, intellectually, institutionally and publicly. *Cultural Studies* hopes to provide a forum for response and strategic discussion.

Cultural Studies assumes that the knowledge formations that make up the field are as historically and geographically contingent as are the determinations of any cultural practice or configuration and that the work produced within or at its permeable boundaries will be diverse. We hope not only to represent but to enhance this diversity. Consequently, we encourage submissions from various disciplinary, theoretical and geographical perspectives, and hope to reflect the wide-ranging articulations, both global and local, among historical, political, economic, cultural and everyday discourses. At the heart of these articulations are questions of community, identity, agency and change.

We expect to publish work that is politically and strategically driven, empirically grounded, theoretically sophisticated, contextually defined and reflexive about its status, however critical, within the range of cultural studies. *Cultural Studies* is about theorizing politics and politicizing theory. How this is to be accomplished in any context remains, howevever, open to rigorous enquiry. As we look towards the future of the field and the journal, it is this enquiry that we especially hope to support.

Lawrence Grossberg
Della Pollock *January 1998*

Contents

VOLUME 12 NUMBER 1 JANUARY 1998

Judith Farquhar, Tomoko Masuzawa and Carol Mavor

A NOTE FROM THE EDITORS

> The famous Rue du Caire at the 1889 Paris exhibition reproduced an entire street of the Egyptian capital, and imported real Egyptian donkeys and their drivers. By its realism, the artificial proclaims itself to be not the real. The very scale and accuracy of the model assure the visitor that there must exist some original of which this is a mere copy. Such techniques persuade one not that the representation is necessarily exact, but that there is a pure reality out there, untouched by the forms of displacement, intermediation, and repetition that render the image merely an image.
>
> (Timothy Mitchell, *Colonising Egypt*)

THE LOGIC OF REPRESENTATION, understood as a presence standing for an absence which authorizes it, has been nearly coterminous with the epistemic domain of the modern West. From the notion of political representation in liberal democracies to linguistic theories of the sign, from the representationalism of realist art and literature to the truth claims of scientific modelling, this logic has pervaded our languages and debates without, until recently, drawing much attention to itself in scholarly literature. As the power, ubiquity and necessity of representation has been taken for granted for centuries, we have tended to assume that the only substantive problem of representation has to do with false, biased, or unfair images. It has seemed that the task of the critic has been to correct the moral and cognitive depravities of words and pictures in an effort to replace untruthful representations with more accurate ones.

Recent studies in diverse fields in the humanities and social sciences have come to question these assumptions in a number of ways. The emerging critical discourse about representation is less concerned with the accuracy of images and statements than it is with the examination of the power of representation as a historically specific ideology and practice endemic to the globalizing politics – and increasingly global reach – of the modern West. A commonly shared objective here, one might say, is not so much to 'fix' this or that bad representation as to unhinge to a degree the obsessively compelling logic of representation as such.

This type of critique – as reflected in all of the articles collected here – often takes the form of *dislocation* in the interest of *articulation*.

Thoroughgoing critiques of representation, seen as a historically contingent logic and practice, are by now well advanced on a number of fronts. Perhaps more significantly, wherever such critical endeavours take place, the established disciplinary divisions and boundaries are not respected; this has been the case despite the apparently growing insularity of academic disciplines in North America. The inherently transgressive interdisciplinarity of the critique of representation, to be sure, is not a mere extension of the age-old striving for the unity of science. Indeed, positivist attempts to rank all the 'sciences' in nested and ultimately reconcilable accounts of a single world seem increasingly quaint in the context of the twentieth-century growth of incommensurate disciplinary idioms. Meanwhile, the development of a common language of critical theory has crossed academic divisions in such ways as to inform new work in fields as remote from each other as art and physics, sociology and literature. A conversation is taking place between and beyond academic departments. This collection of articles is a product of and a contribution to that conversation.

The articles gathered in this volume are theoretically informed empirical studies which contribute to the unfixing of representational logic and technologies from an array of disciplinary perspectives. Together, they demonstrate a variety of ways in which theoretically informed scholarship can engage in the examination of historical and contemporary representational practices in a materialist and critical mode.

This volume grew out of a two-day conference we organized together in 1994, entitled *(Un)Fixing Representation*, held on the campus of the University of North Carolina, Chapel Hill. The conference was funded by the Program in Social Theory and Cross-Cultural Studies (subsequently incorporated into the newly established University Program in Cultural Studies), the Institute for the Arts and Humanities, Office of the Vice Chanceller for Graduate Studies and Research, Office of the Dean of the College of Arts and Sciences, and the Department of Art. We gratefully acknowledge these academic and administrative units of the University for their support, and we thank all those who participated in the conference in varying capacities.

Peter Stallybrass

'WELL GRUBBED, OLD MOLE': MARX, *HAMLET*, AND THE (UN)FIXING OF REPRESENTATION

Abstract

In the *Eighteenth Brumaire*, Marx pursues a double strategy: history is represented, on the one hand, as a catastrophic decline from Napoleon to Louis Bonaparte; while on the other, this 'debased' repetition is depicted as unsettling the notion of a heroic past. Napoleon I can now be read back through his nephew: his ghost is reawakened, but as a caricature. Yet caricature, parody, satire, and farce were far from negative forms for Marx. They were indeed the necessary forms of representation in a society where 'an epic ... can no longer be written'. In the *Eighteenth Brumaire*, Marx developed a brilliant if unsystematic account of literary and political representation and of repetition as the unsettling of origins. He did this, above all, through a direct and indirect rereading of Hamlet as parody or farce, in which the dead father is rewritten as an 'old mole'.

Keywords Marx; Hamlet; repetition; farce; mole

In December 1851, Louis Bonaparte staged a *coup d'état* in Paris and seized control of the state. Marx immediately set to work to write weekly articles for intended publication by his friend, Joseph Weydemeyer, in a German language publication in New York. The publication history of *The Eighteenth Brumaire* (which Marx himself emphasizes) runs counter to Engels' account in his Preface to its third German edition of 1885. In his Preface, Engels rewrites Marx's journalism within the oeuvre of Marx's earlier theory of the modes of production, outlined in *The German Ideology*. *The Eighteenth Brumaire* merely confirms 'the law according to which all historical struggles, whether they proceed in the political, the religious, philosophical or some other domain, are in fact only the more or less clear expression of struggles of social classes' (14). For Engels, what is most striking about Marx's occasional writing of 1851 is that it overrides all contingency to grasp the 'ephemeral' aspect of political occasion as the indirect representation of an already known social conjuncture. On Engels' account, the events of 1851 'never took [Marx] by surprise' (14). Engels was, of course, writing after the fall of the Second Empire, and from that perspective, Marx's narrative could be represented as an omniscient analysis of historical teleology.

But there is an extraordinary disparity between Engels' Preface in 1885 and Marx's Preface to the second edition of 1869. Where Engels claims that Marx was never taken by surprise, Marx's own Preface stages the radical contingencies by which his representation of the events of 1851 came (or rather failed to come) to public attention. Marx's essays were intended for what was to be a German language political weekly, published in New York, beginning on 1 January 1852. But Wedermeyer never won sufficient financial backing for his journal, so the weekly never appeared. Instead, Wedermeyer proposed printing a monthly called *Die Revolution*, although this too ran into financial difficulties and collapsed after the second issue. The first issue of the journal consisted of Marx's *Eighteenth Brumaire*. Some 1000 copies of the journal were printed, one-third of which were sent from the US back to Europe. But booksellers refused to handle the journal, and those that circulated at all were distributed by friends and sympathizers (Mehring, 218). The work itself, Marx claims, 'took shape under the immediate pressure of events' (7) and even the republication in 1869 is due to local circumstances: 'in part to the demand of the book trade, in part to the urgent request of my friends in Germany' (7). Marx's text, in other words, far from existing as a stable representation, was itself, as Marx insists, shaped by economic and political contingencies.

One small trace of these contingencies is inscribed in the change to the book's title: when it was printed in 1852 in *Die Revolution*, its title was *Der Achtzehnte Brumaire des Louis Napoleon*; in 1869 it is *The Eighteenth Brumaire of Louis Bonaparte*. The change is a small one but striking none the less, and itself suggests Marx's acute attention to historical contingency, the uncertainties which Engels attempted to erase. When Marx first published *The Eighteenth Brumaire*, Louis Bonaparte had not yet assumed the official title of Emperor, which he only did in December 1852. As Emperor, he became Napoleon III. To retain the earlier title of the book would be to grant a seeming legitimacy to Louis's claim to the name Napoleon. In this new conjuncture, Marx needed to assert the *illegitimacy* of Louis Bonaparte's assumption of the name, and legacy, of his uncle. He did this by insisting on the family name, Bonaparte, rather than Napoleon. There is a further twist, of which, it seems, Marx was not aware. Even Napoleon I had only a contingent relation to his own name. For his father, Carlo Maria, had decided to name his first three sons after his great-grandfather's sons: the first, Joseph; the second, Napoleon (Nabulion); the third, Lucien. When Napoleon Bonaparte was born, he was christened Lucien. But the eldest brother, Joseph, died. So the father decided to shift the names of the remaining sons up one. Thus, the son who had been christened Napoleon became Joseph; and the son who had been christened Lucien became Napoleon. The Napoleon who ruled France and gave his name to a legal code was first named Lucien and only later Napoleon. The stability of Napoleon I's claim to his own name was no more secure than that of Napoleon III.

A conjunctural understanding of history necessarily emphasizes the contingencies which are dressed up as historical inevitability. But in *The Eighteenth Brumaire*, while Marx proposes such a conjunctural interpretation, he also suggests that the present necessarily works through the assumption of the *magics* of the past: the names (Napoleon), the ideas (empire), the clothes and emblems. Hence, the much quoted opening to *The Eighteenth Brumaire*:

> Hegel remarks somewhere that all facts and all personages of great importance in world history occur, as it were, twice. He forgot to add: the first time as tragedy, the second as farce. (15)

Any synchronic view of history, in other words, must attend to the ways in which the past haunts the present. Representation itself depends upon *belatedness*, a coming after. We dress ourselves, whether we want to or not, in the clothes of the past:

> The tradition of all the dead generations weighs like a nightmare on the brain of the living. And just when they seem engaged in revolutionizing themselves and things, in creating something that has never yet existed, precisely in such periods of revolutionary crisis they anxiously conjure up the spirits of the past to their service and borrow from them names, battle cries and costumes in order to present the new scene of world history in this time-honoured disguise and this borrowed language. (15)

The contingencies of the new are represented through the 'borrowed languages' of the past: Luther clothes himself as the Apostle Paul; Cromwell assumes the guise of Old Testament prophet; the Revolution of 1789 to 1814 drapes itself alternately as the Roman Republic and the Roman Empire.

Marx appears at first to raise the problem of the repetition of the past to distinguish between the 'heroic' bourgeois revolutions of the seventeenth and eighteenth centuries and the reactionary *coup d'état* of Louis Bonaparte. In contrast, the 'revolution' of Louis Bonaparte is a farcical repetition, a mere parody of the past, an awakening of the dead only to travesty them. In place of Danton and Robespierre, Caussidière and Louis Blanc; in place of the Montagne of 1793, the Montagne of 1848; in place of *The Eighteenth Brumaire* of Napoleon I, the *coup d'état* of his nephew, an adventurer 'who hides his commonplace repulsive features under the iron death mask of Napoleon' (17).

But this opposition between the 'tragedies' of early bourgeois upheavals and the 'farce' of their later simulations is unsettled by Marx's acknowledgement that even those early upheavals only *used* tragedy as one of 'the ideals and the art forms, the self deceptions that they needed in order to conceal from themselves the bourgeois limitations of the content of their struggles' (16). '[T]he high plane of the great historical tragedy' is *itself*, then, a repetition in which a society as 'unheroic as bourgeois society' dresses itself up (16–17). Only after the revolution can bourgeois society assume its 'true' guise: not Habakkuk but Locke. To put it another way, the classical hierarchy of genres, in which tragedy was considered the most elevated and farce the most debased of genres, can no longer retain its unquestioned status within a bourgeois society that pursues the 'novel'. Tragedy must now itself be understood as farce. From this perspective, Louis Bonaparte is the most appropriate of performers upon the stage of bourgeois society, for he unintentionally unmasks the self-deceptions of the elevated genres through which an earlier bourgeois society imagined itself. In Marx's words, Louis Bonaparte produces 'not only a caricature of the old Napoleon,' but also 'the old Napoleon himself, caricatured as he must appear in the middle of the nineteenth century' (18). And Marx's Preface to the second edition makes clear his own desire to submit the cult of the first Napoleon to 'the weapons of historical research, of criticism, of satire and of wit' (8).

Marx thus pursues a double strategy in *The Eighteenth Brumaire*. Through the first strategy, history is represented as a catastrophic decline from Napoleon to Louis Bonaparte. But in the second strategy, the effect of this 'debased' repetition is to unsettle the status of the origin. Napoleon I can now only be read back through his nephew: his ghost is awakened but as a caricature. Yet caricature, parody, satire and farce were far from negative forms for Marx. They were indeed the necessary forms of representation in a society where 'an epic . . . can no longer be written' (Prawer, 15). Marx, in *The Eighteenth Brumaire*, developed a brilliant if unsystematic account of literary and political representation and of repetition and the settling and unsettling of origins. He did this above all through an indirect rereading of *Hamlet* as parody or farce.

Let me begin by emphasizing Marx's profound interest both in Shakespeare and in parodic forms. In 1837, as a young man of 19, Marx began work on *Scorpion und Felix*, a comic novel. Its structure and techniques were based not upon the *bildungsroman* of Goethe but upon Sterne's 'anti-novel', *Tristram Shandy*, for which Marx had the highest admiration. Like Sterne, Marx delighted in 'sudden, deliberate let-downs' and in 'verbal cartoons' (Prawer, 15). Like Sterne, Marx developed a range of parodies: of The Bible, of Ovid, of Goldsmith's *The Vicar of Wakefield*, but above all of Shakespeare. Not only does Marx parody Shakespeare, and in particular *Richard III*, but he also pays particular attention to parody *in* Shakespeare, and to the bitter fool Thersites in *Troilus and Cressida*, a fool whom Marx would continue to quote and to appropriate throughout his life.

Shakespeare was Marx's favourite author, as he was to become his daughters'. Marx had learned his love for Shakespeare in the 1830s from Ludwig von Westphalen, soon to be his father-in-law. Eleanor, Marx's daughter, later wrote that 'whereas [Marx's] father read Voltaire and Racine with him, the Baron [von Westphalen] read him Homer and Shakespeare – who remained his favourite authors all his life' (McLellan, 1973: 15). But it was particularly when he moved to England in 1849, and in his earlier visits, that Marx devoted himself to Shakespeare, whom he read every day. As Franz Mehring wrote in his memoir of Marx:

> After Marx had become permanently domiciled in London, English literature took first place, and the tremendous figure of Shakespeare dominated the field; in fact the whole family practiced what amounted practically to a Shakespearean cult.
>
> (*Literature and Art*, 143)

When they moved to London, the Marxes would frequently take a picnic to Hampstead Heath on Sundays. On the way out, according to their fellow exile, Wilhelm Liebkneckt, they would sing African-American spirituals; on their return, Karl and his wife Jenny would recite whole scenes from Shakespeare. Eleanor Marx, in her recollections of her father, wrote:

> As to Shakespeare he was the Bible of our house, seldom out of our hands or mouths. By the time I was six I knew scene upon scene of Shakespeare by heart.
>
> (Baxandall and Morawski, 149)

Eleanor aspired to being a Shakespearean actor, and later became a keen member of Furnivall's New Shakespeare Society. She and her sister Jenny also wrote a series of articles on Shakespeare for the *Frankfurter Zeitung*. Towards the end of Marx's life, Shakespeare play readings were held at Marx's house by a group who called themselves the Dogberry Club (Fedoseyev, 518).

But this devotion to Shakespeare scarcely suggests just *what* Marx admired in him, which was precisely the hybridity that had led Voltaire to call Shakespeare a drunken savage. In opposition to Voltaire, Marx praised Shakespearean drama for 'its peculiar mixture of the sublime and the base, the terrible and the ridiculous, the heroic and the burlesque' (Prawer, 241). After 1848, according to Paul Lafargue, Marx 'sought out . . . all the peculiar expressions used by Shakespeare', and if this was in part to extend his command of English, it was also because he took particular pleasure in the Shakespearean grotesque: in Falstaff, in Thersites, in the base and the farcical. He was, as Lafargue remarks, interested in 'the *peculiar* expressions', as he was interested in the '*peculiar* mixture' of Shakespearean drama. It was, in other words, the very *im*purities of Shakespearean drama, its resistance to a classical theory of representation, which interested Marx. It was a similar fascination with the hybrid which led Marx to call his book in response to the libels of Karl Vogt, *Da-Da Vogt*. Da-Da was the name given to a translator of Bonapartist pamphlets circulating in Algeria. Although Marx's family and friends persuaded him to discard the title as too obscure, he did so reluctantly. The name 'Da-Da', he wrote, 'puzzles the philistine and is comical'; it 'fits well into my system of mockery and contempt' (Prawer, 265). Marx thus pre-empted the dadaists' subversion of representation by more than half a century.

The farcical in Marx, though, is not only used as part of his 'system of mockery and contempt'; it is equally central to his system of celebration. And it is here that Marx works against the pathos of decline ('then, they were giants;

now, we are dwarves') which would be one way of reading the opening sentences of *The Eighteenth Brumaire*: history repeats itself, the first time as tragedy, the realm of heroes, the second time as farce, the realm of buffoons and scoundrels. For Marx, though, if Da-Da Vogt can only be represented through the grotesque, proletarian revolution must be represented equally unheroically:

> proletarian revolutions . . . criticize themselves constantly, interrupt themselves continuously in their own course, come back to the apparently accomplished in order to begin it afresh, deride with unmerciful thoroughness the inadequacies, weaknesses and paltrinesses of their first attempts, seem to throw down their adversary only in order that he may draw new strength from the earth and rise again, more gigantic, before them, recoil ever and anon from the indefinite prodigiousness of their own aims, until a situation has been created which makes all turning back impossible, and the conditions themselves cry out:
> *Hic Rhodus, hic salta!*
> *Here is the rose, here dance!*

For Marx, the features of the coming revolution will be hesitancy, an awareness of inadequacy, and it is imagined in the realm of fairy-tale (the giant who is knocked down only to gain more power) and of *Aesop's Fables*. ('Here is Rhodes, leap here!' is taken from Aesop's tale 'The Swaggerer', in which a boaster who claims that he made an enormous leap in Rhodes is mockingly asked to repeat the leap from where he is right now.)

Just as Marx adopts contradictory techniques to represent Louis Bonaparte as simultaneously a shrunken parody of his heroic uncle *and* as the unmasking of the impossibility of any heroism (whether Napoleon I's or Napoleon III's) within the categories of bourgeois society, so Marx adopts contradictory techniques to represent revolution. On the one hand, it is, he claims, unrepresentable ('the social revolution of the nineteenth century cannot draw its poetry from the past'; 'the content goes beyond the phrase'); on the other, he himself represents it through two odd appropriations of 'poetry from the past': the revolution is Puck or Robin Goodfellow from *A Midsummer Night's Dream*; it is the ghost of Hamlet's father. These two latter images are combined by Marx in a speech he delivered on 14 April 1856, on the anniversary of the Chartist *People's Paper*. Here he stages a curious paradox: what he calls 'the new-fangled forces of society' create people who are so novel that they can no longer be grasped through prior systems of representation. The working men and women of the nineteenth century are, Marx declares, 'as much the invention of modern times as machinery itself' (Prawer, 246). Yet Marx himself immediately defines this revolutionary moment through those very past languages which he has implicitly rejected:

> In the signs that bewilder the middle class, the aristocracy and the poor prophets of regression, we recognize our brave friend, Robin Goodfellow,

> the old mole that can work in the earth so fast, that worthy pioneer – the Revolution.
>
> (*Articles on Britain*, 262–3)

Marx, in other words, imagines revolution both as an epistemic break which, having 'stripped off all superstition in regard to the past', turns its back upon the past so as to constitute itself in and through the future; and as parodic repetition, a repetition presided over by the ghosts of the past.

The Eighteenth Brumaire, indeed, is not only a reworking of *Hamlet* but also of Marx's own attitude towards ghosts and haunting. Much of his earlier writing had been dedicated to the exorcism of ghosts, whether conjured up by religion or by Hegel. In the first section of *The Eighteenth Brumaire*, Marx retains a distinction between 'mere' ghosts and 'true' spirits: the awakening of the dead in earlier revolutions 'served the purpose of glorifying the new struggles, not of parodying the old; of magnifying the given task in imagination, not of fleeing from its solution in reality; of finding once more the spirit of revolution, not of making its ghost walk about again' (17). Ghosts are a superstition, a drug (18); the dead must be left to bury the dead. Yet in the final section of *The Eighteenth Brumaire*, as in the opening of *The Communist Manifesto*, the radicalized proletariat itself erupts as a ghost: 'A spectre is haunting Europe'; 'Well grubbed, old mole!'. In the imagined proletarian revolution, as in the February Revolution which Marx denounces, a 'prophecy' 'haunts the subsequent acts of the drama like a ghost' (118).

But the ghosts which Marx invokes are not heroic. Indeed, when he invokes them, they are as parodic as Louis Bonaparte. Marx's prophetic ghosts are Robin Goodfellow or Puck; the ghost of Hamlet's father but in the form of 'the old mole that can work in the earth so fast, that worthy pioneer'. It is the latter figure upon whom I shall concentrate here. In his speech of 1856, Marx is himself repeating his writing of 1852. In *The Eighteenth Brumaire*, he had written of the seeming defeat of socialism by Louis Bonaparte's *coup*:

> The struggle seems to be settled in such a way that all classes, equally impotent and equally mute, fall on their knees before the rifle butt.
>
> But the revolution is thoroughgoing. It is still journeying through purgatory. It does its work methodically. . . . And when it has done this second half of its preliminary work, Europe will leap from its seat and exultantly exclaim: Well grubbed, old mole! (*Brav gewühlt, alter Maulwurf!*)
>
> (121; vol. 11, 178)

But why does Marx represent the revolution through the ghost of Hamlet's father? And, even more to the point, why does he invoke that ghost (and the revolution) in Hamlet's grotesque and debasing image of his father as a *mole*?

Let me first outline as clearly as possible my major suppositions in my understanding of the relation between Marx's analysis of Louis Bonaparte and his reading of *Hamlet*. To repeat what I have already argued: the period from

1848–52 saw Marx engaged both in a detailed analysis of French politics and the rise of Louise Bonaparte and in an intense reading of Shakespeare. These two concerns, I believe, complexly converge in *The Eighteenth Brumaire*, which is, like *Hamlet*, an analysis of repetition. While the nephew, Napoleon III-to-be, farcically repeats his uncle, Napoleon I, Hamlet, the son, assumes an 'antic disposition' and farcically repeats his father, Hamlet. Both narratives depend upon the repetition of a name (Napoleon, Hamlet); both, at least temporarily, conjure up a previously tragic world which has been displaced by a farcical one. Both texts explore how the past haunts the present, and how the past is trans

But if the past haunts the present, it is also *re*-presented, transformed by the remaking of its presence. Nowhere is this more striking than in *Hamlet*. Hamlet, the son, obsessively idealizes his father, comparing him as Hyperion, the sun-god, to the satyr of his uncle, Claudius. And when Hamlet, the father, returns, it is in his most heroic form, dressed in armour; and not just any armour, but 'the very armour [he] had on' when he fought and defeated Fortinbras. The father returns, we might say, as the material trace which has survived him: the armour which was a typical legacy from father to son, surviving the father's death to mould, whether literally or ideologically, the son's identity. It was, for instance, 'the remainder of two rich armours which were my father's' which Lady Anne Clifford left to her grandchildren 'to remaine to them and their posterity . . . as a remembrance of him'. Such physical remembrances powerfully fix representation, and it is precisely such a fixing (of his father's memory, of his own assumption of his father's name) that Hamlet desires, as Napoleon III attempted to fix and appropriate the legacy of his uncle.

What Marx takes from *Hamlet*, though, is not Hamlet's attempt to *be* his father but the radical unsettling of this revenance in the son's (un)naming of the paternal legacy. For Hamlet, as for his friends Marcellus, Barnardo and Horatio, the Ghost is at first not 'he' but 'it'. The Ghost is only transformed from 'it' by Hamlet's own act of naming: 'I'll *call* thee Hamlet,/King, father, royal Dane.' And yet, having named his father in the full majesty of his authority, Hamlet proceeds to strip him of those very titles, addressing him with an increasingly mocking familiarity:

> Ah ha, boy, say'st thou so? Art thou there, truepenny?
> Come on, you hear this fellow in the cellarage.

'Boy', 'truepenny', 'fellow': each word debases the father, dethrones the monarch. 'Boy': a male child before puberty; also, in the Renaissance, a servant or slave, and, as a term of contempt, a rogue or knave. 'Truepenny': an honest fellow but a term commonly used patronizingly of an inferior ('Truepenny' is the name of a servant in *Ralph Roister Doister*). 'Fellow': a companion or comrade; but also the customary address of a servant, and with the contemptuous sense of a person of no worth. The King and father no longer enthroned but 'in the cellarage' – beneath the ground but also, in the technical language of the theatre, underneath the stage – literally subordinated, even in his terrifying return.

The father finally as mole:
Well said, old mole. Canst work i' th' earth so fast?
A worthy pioneer!

Hamlet, the dead father, no longer King and royal Dane but mole and pioneer. In appropriating 'old mole' as a figure of revolution, Marx brilliantly illuminates, even as he transforms the politics of the Renaissance play from which he appropriates. For while *Hamlet* seems to contrast the supposed legitimacy of primogeniture – the chain of father and son, Hamlet and Hamlet – with the illegitimate usurpation of the brother/uncle, Claudius, the play, as Marx's appropriation suggests, stages something more unsettling: the transformation of the principle of legitimacy – the father and King – into the principle of subversion. One should take subversion quite literally here. The modern German for subversive activity – *Maulwurfsarbeit* – means literally the work of the mole. In figuring his father as mole, Hamlet enacts a radical metamorphosis: from human to animal; from omnipotent monarch to blind burrower; from ideological figurehead to a worker in the ground. It is a literal humbling, a bringing of the ideological superstructure down to earth (*humus*, the etymological root for 'humble', is the Latin for 'earth').

The transformation of the father into mole has a further unsettling implication. For the word occurs only one other time in *Hamlet*, and that is in the preceding scene, where Hamlet derides the Danish wassails:

So, oft it chances in particular men
That for some vicious mole of nature in them,
As in their birth, wherein they are not guilty
(Since nature cannot choose his origin),
By their o'ergrowth of some complexion,
Oft breaking down the pales and forts of reason,
Or by some habit, that too much o'erleavens
The form of plausive manners – that these men,
Carrying, I say, the stamp of one defect,
Being Nature's livery or Fortunes star,
His virtues else, be they as pure as grace,
As infinite as any man may undergo,
Shall in the general censure take corruption
From that particular fault.

(1. 4: 23–36)

The mole, then, not only as burrowing animal, but as defect, taint, a 'particular fault' which can corrupt the whole. For 'mole' also signifies a discoloured spot on linen ('one iron mole defaceth the whole piece of lawn') and a blemish on the skin ('one mole staineth the whole face'). In *King John*, a mother talks of a child who is 'sland'rous to [his] mother's womb' as one who is '[p]atch'd with foul moles and eye-offending marks' (3. 1: 43), and when Oberon concludes *A Midsummer Night's Dream* with a blessing upon the betrothed couples, he says:

> So shall all the couples three
> Ever true in loving be;
> And the blots of Nature's hand
> Shall not in their issue stand;
> Never mole, hare-lip, nor scar,
> Nor mark prodigious, such as are
> Despised in nativity,
> Shall upon their children be.
>
> (5. 1: 407)

In figuring his father as 'old mole', Hamlet associates him with the 'blots of Nature' which subvert legitimacy and unfix the patrilineal bond, and he begins the process by which he will, despite his repeated promises to 'remember' his father, reject the suit of armour which would remake him in his father's image.

For if Hamlet takes upon himself the Ghost's demand, if he is buried as a soldier with '[t]he soldier's music, and the rites of war', he never becomes his armoured father. Indeed, when Hamlet returns from England, he writes to Claudius in a curiously ambiguous phrase that he is '*set naked on your kingdom*'. His farcical representation of his father as mole precedes his putting on of an 'antic disposition', the disposition of the fool or court jester. And it is the court jester, Yorick, not his father, whom Hamlet most fondly recalls: 'he hath born me on his back a thousand times, and now – how abhorred in my imagination it is. My gorge rises at it. Here hung those lips that I have kissed I know not how oft.' The lips that he has kissed: the lips not of the father but of the jester. Though Yorick is dead, his skull memorializes the legacy he leaves, a legacy which includes the 'antic disposition'. In striking contrast to *The Spanish Tragedy*, where the Ghost returns gloatingly to conclude the plot, the Ghost of *Hamlet* simply disappears after Act 3. One might say that the Ghost of the jester displaces the Ghost of the soldier-king.

However, if we are to believe the so-called 'bad' first quarto of *Hamlet*, the soldier-king had been displaced even before Act 3. In the bedchamber scene, as Hamlet berates his mother, the stage direction reads, 'Enter the ghost in his night gowne.' A king no longer clad in complete steel but in the robes of undress, ready for bed. A supposedly heroic past subverted by this revelation of domestic vulnerability. It is not clear to whom Hamlet refers when he says 'a king of shreds and patches': to his usurping uncle or to his father, stripped of the trappings of power – boy, truepenny, fellow, old mole. Marx himself opens the way for such an absorption of the legitimating father/King into the delegitimating fool and jester in his own reworking of the 'old mole' for his speech of 1856, quoted above:

> In the signs that bewilder the middle class, the aristocracy and the poor prophets of regression, we recognize our brave friend, Robin Goodfellow,

> the old mole that can work in the earth so fast, that worthy pioneer – the Revolution.
>
> (*Articles on Britain*, 262–3)

Hamlet, the father/King, as Puck; Puck, like 'Da-Da', as the bewilderer of the bourgeoisie.

In his 1856 speech, Marx extends his previous quotation of *Hamlet*: it is the 'old mole', he continues, 'that can work in the earth so fast, that worthy pioneer'. *This* mole, the 'spectre [which] is haunting Europe' in the opening sentence of *The Communist Manifesto* is 'a pioneer', a word which ironically combines both the sense of a rupture with the past and the sense of the historical conditions 'which weigh like a nightmare on the brain of the living'. By the 1830s, the metaphorical sense of a pioneer as explorer or initiator had taken on a specific reference in the United States. In 1836, Irving wrote: 'As one wave of emigration after another rolls into the vast regions of the waste, the eager eyes of our pioneers will pry beyond.' In this sense, the Revolution is imagined as opening up an unforeseen future. But such a future, for Marx, could only be constructed upon the specific labours of the past and the present. A 'pioneer' in the older sense is less glamorous, more a mole, 'one of a body of foot-soldiers who march with or in advance of an army or regiment, having spaces, pickaxes etc. to dig trenches, repair roads, and perform other labours in clearing and preparing the way for the main body'; also, by extension, a miner.

The Eighteenth Brumaire reads *Hamlet* as a staging of the unfixing of representation. Yet that unfixing itself depends upon repetition. Marx's 'mole', indeed, repeats not only *Hamlet* but the conclusion of Hegel's *Lectures on the Philosophy of History*, where Hegel argued that 'the latest philosophy contains therefore those which went before . . . it is the product and result of all that preceded it' (Hegel, 552–3; 690–1). 'Individuals', though, cannot stand outside that process so as to grasp it; they are themselves 'like blind men, who are driven forward by the indwelling spirit of the whole'. But the spirit can only emerge 'into the light of day' if we 'give ear to its urgency – when the mole that is within forces its way on – and we have to make it a reality' (553; 691). But Marx's mole, unlike Hegel's, is not working towards the light; it is working in the earth. Its labour is one of uprooting. Indeed, in Marx's rematerialization of the work of the Ghost, he *mis*quotes *Hamlet*. In F1, the lines are:

> Well said old Mole, can'st worke i'th'ground so fast? A worthy Pioneer.

Or, in the Schlegel/Tieck translation which Marx also knew:

> Brav, alter Maulwurf! Wühlst so hurtig fort? O trefflicher Minierer!
>
> (*Hamlet*, Prinz von Dänemark in *Shakspeare: Dramatische Werke*, trans. August Wilhelm von Schlegel and Ludwig Tieck (Berlin: Reimer, 1841, vol. 6: 35))

In *The Eighteenth Brumaire*, though, 'Well *said*, old mole' becomes 'well *grubbed*, old mole' (Brav *gewühlt, alter Maulwurf*): the mouth as organ of speech becomes the mouth as organ of eating. Hamlet, the father, no longer as *paterfamilias*, no longer even as absent command ('well said') but as grubber-up, as delegitimator.

For Marx, the repetition of the name 'Hamlet' itself covers a double dislocation: the dislocation of the father from palace to cellarage; the dislocation of the father's legacy and its displacement by that of Yorick and Puck. Yet unfixing itself depends upon repetition, a repetition which can never be totally detached from fixation. Fixation cannot be erased; it is itself the site of transformation. Marx stages both fixation and transformation in his own repetitive rereadings of Shakespeare, in his development of Hamlet's transformation of monarch into mole into miner into Puck. In the unnaming of the patriarch, Marx perhaps found intimations for his radically incomplete interrogation of his own paternal position. When Eleanor, his daughter, wrote her memoir of him, she called it *Recollections of Mohr [the Moor]*. Mohr, Challey, Old Nick, were the names by which his family called him, names which dislocate the comic Marx from the tragedy of his frozen legacy. The title 'Old Mole' was reserved not for kings and patriarchs, but for the Revolution – and for a woman, an intimate family friend named Lina Schüler (E. Marx, 634).

I want to conclude with a more recent reworking of the 'old mole' – that of Hélène Cixous in *Sorties*:

> So all the history, all the stories would be there to retell differently; the future would be incalculable; the historic forces would and will change hands and change body – another thought which is as yet unthinkable – will transform the functioning of all society. We are living in an age where the conceptual foundations of an ancient culture is in the process of being undermined by millions of a species of mole (Topoi, ground mines) never known before. When they wake up from among the dead, from among words, from among laws. (65)

The mole itself has changed hands, has changed bodies: from Shakespeare's ungendered 'mole' to Marx's masculine *Maulwurf* to Cixous's feminine *taupe* – the French for mole, landmine, but also, historically, for prostitute and old hag (*vieille taupe*). But the moles which will unfix representation are also, in Cixous's lexicon, *topoi*, commonplaces – like the mole itself, the site simultaneously of cultural repetition and of social dislocation. We make history in our reworking of borrowed names, borrowed cities, borrowed costumes (65).

Patrick Brantlinger

FORGETTING GENOCIDE: OR, THE LAST OF *THE LAST OF THE MOHICANS*

Abstract

In the wake of the 1992 debates about Columbus, the discovery of the Americas, and whether terms such as 'holocaust', 'genocide', and 'racism' should be applied to what happened to Native Americans, Michael Mann's film remake of James Fenimore Cooper's *The Last of the Mohicans* continues a process of historical erasure or forgetting that Cooper and his contemporaries began. The sentimental racism expressed in Cooper's novel involves the ideas of the auto-genocide of 'savagery' and the inevitable extinction of all Native Americans – ideas commonly held about other so-called primitive races in other imperialist contexts (for instance, about the Maoris of New Zealand). Though Mann purported to take great pains in his film to be historically accurate, the film is only accurate in relation to trivial details. It thoroughly scrambles major aspects of Cooper's text, including converting the ageing Natty Bumppo into a young sex-symbol (Daniel Day-Lewis). More importantly, the film completely erases Cooper's sentimental racism by, for instance, turning Chingachgook rather than his son, Uncas, into the 'last' of his tribe, and thereby overlooking the motif of the futureless child central to that racism. But in eliminating Cooper's racism, the film in a sense perfects the novel, because the sentimentalism that softened the racism was already a form of erasure or forgetting.

Keywords Native Americans; genocide; racism; imperialism; historical forgetting or erasure

> Cooper is not a close observer, but he is . . . interesting. . . . And he is more interesting when he is not noticing what he is about than when he is.
>
> (Mark Twain)

> The plaintiff complains that he has been fooled about the existence of gas chambers, fooled that is, about the so-called Final Solution. His argument is: in order for a place to be identified as a gas chamber, the only eyewitness I will accept would be a victim of this gas chamber; now . . . there is no victim that is not dead. . . . There is, therefore, no gas chamber.
>
> (Lyotard, *The Differend (*1988))

HOW MANY ACTS OF FORGETTING are necessary for the official or semi-official history of a modern nation-state? Debates sparked by 1992's revisionary histories of Columbus and the Americas are especially resonant in relation to debates about just how unique or extreme was the Nazi Holocaust, and indeed about whether there even was a holocaust. Thus in reviewing several of the 1992 books for *NYRB*, including David Stannard's *American Holocaust*, J. H. Elliott declares that 'holocaust', 'genocide' and even 'racism' are an 'emotive vocabulary' of 'moral outrage' inappropriate in describing what really happened to Native Americans. Needless to say, Native American authors are not as worried about using 'emotive' terms like 'genocide' as is Professor Elliott (see, for instance, Churchill, and also the essays in Jaimes). Moreover, in relation to *wie es eigentlich gewesen* to Native America, several recent films seem resonant, including Michael Mann's remake of Cooper's *The Last of the Mohicans*.[1]

In a *Newsweek* article about the opening of the United States Holocaust Museum in Washington, DC, Kenneth Woodward asks but does not quite answer: 'Why memorialize *this* singular, Godforsaken episode in Jewish history when we still have no building recalling what the United States did to Native Americans or to its African slaves?' Of course there are private and sometimes state-operated museums and historic sites that deal with slavery or with the decimation of native Americans. There just isn't any official 'pyramid of skulls' (Slotkin 1973: 517) in the nation's capital telling either of these stories. Woodward's question points to the official forgetting or trivializing of the two biggest embarrassments to American patriotism. If we should memorialize the Nazi Holocaust in order to remind ourselves that that series of crimes against humanity really happened, and in order to remind ourselves that we should not stand idly by to let it happen again in, say, Bosnia, then surely there is every reason to memorialize the two major genocides which, far from being just embarrassing anomalies, were cornerstones of the new, war-making, imperialistic nation-state that emerged from the cocoon of British imperialism in 1776.

It may be 'emotive', but 'imperialism' is the right name for the United States' westward march to the Pacific, in the course of which countless Native

Americans, like countless bison and passenger pigeons, were slaughtered. And imperialism is also the name for the slave-trade and the plantation economy that slavery built. In both cases, genocide or holocaust are also appropriate, albeit 'emotive', names.[2] Further, perhaps Professor Elliott has forgotten that, quite apart from mass slaughter, the 1948 UN Convention on Genocide includes the concept of cultural genocide, involving any attempt by one social group to eradicate the identity of another – as happened, of course, to those slaves who survived the Middle Passage, and as has happened to greater or lesser extent to Native American survivors of their holocaust.[3] But what about eradicating or forgetting aspects of the victors' culture, like the racism – another 'emotive' word – that helps to legitimize genocide?

The opening of the United States Holocaust Museum occurred while the recent film version of *The Last of the Mohicans* was showing in local theatres. I saw the movie at just about this time; it had been a while since I'd read Cooper's novel, but I remembered it well enough to know that the movie is very different, despite claims by its director to have remade the novel *Wie es eigentlich gewesen*. This claim itself, however, is one way in which the movie plays fast and loose with historical memory. In one sense, the movie follows Cooper's text faithfully, because Cooper himself was inventing ways to alter history, above all by making it seem that the extinction of all Native Americans was inevitable. Mann's film *perfects* Cooper's sentimental racism by obliterating that racism (and with it the imperialist/racist roots of US nation-building). Mann is thus also perfecting Cooper's canonization as a classic American author – a canonization rendered possible only through the at least partial cover-up of Cooper's sentimental racism.[4]

> Where are the blossoms of those summers! – fallen, one by one: so all of my family departed . . . to the land of spirits. I am on the hill-top, and must go down into the valley; and when Uncas follows in my footsteps, there will no longer be any of the blood of the sagamores, for my boy is the last of the Mohicans. (28)

So says Chingachgook, sounding the *ubi sunt* theme early in Cooper's novel. By the end of the story, however, Uncas precedes Chingachgook 'into the valley' of death, slain by the evil Huron Magua. The death of the son rather than of the father reinforces the sense of finality: for the Mohican 'race', to use the term Cooper prefers to 'tribe', this is also the death of the future. The future will not even contain half-breed Mohicans, assuming that Uncas might have mated with a non-Mohican like the hybrid Cora, the dark daughter of Colonel Munro.

Because her West Indian blood is tinged with the blood of slaves through her mixed-race mother (159), Cora is attractive both to Magua, who kidnaps her for his wife, and to Uncas. She is an example of the 'tragic mulatta' figure in American literature; but the future of any 'race' for Cooper lies not through miscegenation. Racial as opposed to cultural identity depends upon a fantasy of purity, of unmixed blood. Natty Bumppo as a 'man without a cross' is a man without a *racial* 'cross' or mixture with his Mohican adoptive family.[5] It is above all this fantasy of racial purity that makes Cooper's Leatherstocking novels racist: the fantasy involves the ideas that there is a natural (not culturally constructed) hierarchy of 'races'; that the sexual intermingling of 'races' is wrong or unnatural, because it can only degrade the superior without improving the inferior; and also that certain inferior 'races' like the Mohicans (or like all Indians) are doomed to extinction by some innate flaw – the flaw identical to 'savagery' itself.

Miscegenation from such a racist perspective can only be tragic; the 'tragic mulatta' – if she isn't sterile – can only degrade, not uplift. Moreover, Cora herself is horrified by the prospect of mating with an Indian. And even though she has done nothing to encourage Magua's attentions, she is slain in the grand finale by one of Magua's warriors just as Uncas is trying to rescue her. Magua then kills Uncas just before Hawkeye kills Magua. This is obviously very different from the movie. For one thing, in the film, it's the blonde, blue-eyed Alice who dies at the end, committing suicide to escape from Magua. For another, it's Chingachgook – played, ironically enough, by Russell Means – rather than Uncas who is identified as the last of the Mohicans. Anyway, Cooper's bloody penultimate chapter ends with the deaths of Cora, Uncas and Magua; the final chapter describes the double funeral, performed by the friendly Delawares, for Cora and Uncas, 'last of the Mohicans'. This funereal last chapter underscores the elegiac character of the entire novel, which is saturated with blood and death – the bloodiest of the Leatherstocking series (its graphic portrayal of violence is one of the few ways in which the movie offers a literal rendering of Cooper's text). In a final passage that echoes his opening *ubi sunt* eloquence, Chingachgook mourns his son: 'Why hast thou left us, pride of the Wapanachki? . . . Thou art gone, youthful warrior. . . . Who that saw thee in battle would believe that thou couldst die!' (344). Chingachgook's opening and closing *ubi sunt* statements serve as symmetrical book-ends between which Cooper narrates a history that, for the Mohicans, goes precisely nowhere.

Cooper's elegy to the Mohicans is, of course, also an epic. Like Scott's fictions in relation to modern Great Britain, Cooper depicts central or typical events – battles, migrations, political conflicts, genocides – in the formation of the new American nation-state. That Cooper chose to write *historical* romances after Scott's manner, with Indians in the role of Scott's defeated Jacobite highlanders, is perhaps anomalous, because according to some early American commentators the new nation was too new to have a history. But obviously it had a pre-revolutionary, pre-national past, which is when Cooper sets his plot. Cooper, like Scott, offers a sort of proleptic history or prophecy by hindsight, according to which – in contrast to the Mohicans who have no history – the whole history of the new nation-state of America lies in the future. The elegiac loss of history experienced by the Mohicans is the negative or Great Zero from which springs the future-perfect, epic history of the United States.[6]

The Last of the Mohicans represents the emergence of the modern US out of the colonial past as the process of defeating those of its enemies who were prior to Britain: namely, the French and their Indian allies. But the French are never much of a factor; at the centre are instead the Indians and their fate, which is already implicit in their racial identity as 'savages'. The extinction of the Mohicans adumbrates the total extinction that Cooper believed was the inevitable future of *all* Indians. In Cooper's fantasy this future is displaced into the past and represented as having always already taken place. Cooper offers a fictional rendition of the common nineteenth-century opinion, expressed, for instance, by Washington Irving, that 'There appears to be a tendency to extinction among all the savage nations, and this tendency would seem to have been in operation among the aboriginals of this country long before the advent of the white men' (158). Cooper may not have shared Irving's view that the Indians were on their way to extinction *before* the arrival of Europeans, but he clearly did believe that they were doomed to extinction *because they were savages*, and he also believed that, no matter how the white man behaved, *savagery* by definition would cause the Indians' doom – their auto-genocide, so to speak. In the 1831 Introduction to *The Last of the Mohicans*, Cooper mentions 'the seemingly inevitable fate of all these people, who disappear before the advances . . . of civilisation, as the verdure of their native forests falls before the nipping frost' (6–7).[7]

The basic formula in Cooper is the same as that in countless imperialist texts: savagery extinguishes savagery.[8] The fantasy of racial suicide or auto-genocide is the most extreme form of blaming the victim through which the liquidation of 'primitive races' by European invaders was and continues to be explained away. Such rationalizations share a number of features, starting with the tautological identification of 'savagery' as the prime or sole cause of the extinction of those who practise 'savage' customs. When 'savagery' is not identified as the cause of racial extinction, with 'civilization' helpless to prevent it, then it is frequently held that some groups of 'savages' at least cannot be civilized, and are thus doomed to fall by the wayside no matter what customs they practise. And 'doomed' is the operative word: a third feature of such rationalizations is to treat the extinction of at least certain primitive peoples as inevitable: no amount of humanitarian sentiment can save them. Finally, axiomatically, these rationalizations identify civilization as good and savagery as evil or, at the very least, as less than good.

All these notions are at work in Andrew Jackson's annual presidential message for 1830, which might almost be read as an explication of Cooper's novel:

> Humanity has often wept over the fate of the aborigines of this country [Jackson declares], and Philanthropy has been long busily employed in devising means to avert it, but its progress has never for a moment been arrested, and one by one have many powerful tribes disappeared from the earth. To follow to the tomb the last of his race and to tread on the graves of extinct nations excite melancholy reflections. But true philanthropy

> reconciles the mind to these vicissitudes as it does to the extinction of one generation to make room for another.
>
> (quoted in Pearce, 1965: 57)

Besides, Jackson continues, 'What good man would prefer a country covered with forests and ranged by a few thousand savages to our extensive Republic, studded with cities, towns, and prosperous farms?' Clearly, though it weeps with Chingachgook over the grave of the last of his race, Philanthropy with a capital 'P' is on the side of civilization. But it is not so clear that Jackson is the best spokesman for Philanthropy; according to Michael Rogin, he 'was the single figure most responsible for Indian destruction in pre-Civil War America'.[9]

For Natty Bumppo – though himself half-savage in behaviour – savagery is almost synonymous with evil, even while it is also almost synonymous with a state of nature that equals the innocence of childhood.[10] While Natty can insist that the 'savage warfare' he and his Mohican allies are engaged in is an 'evil [that] has been mainly done by men with white skins', he adds that 'it has ended in turning the tomahawk of brother against brother' (227). Between Chingachgook's early *ubi sunt* pronouncement and the funereal last chapter, the story is crowded with battle scenes which largely involve Indians killing Indians – brother against brother – just as in the grand finale, when Magua kills Uncas. True, the main occasion for warfare is the conflict between the French and the British for the territory around Lake George. But apart from the siege and surrender of Fort William Henry, the French and British conflict hardly seems important. What is in the foreground is quite specifically Indian warfare, announced as such in the opening paragraph: the 'colonial wars of North America' were fought in 'the wilderness' with the techniques of 'the practised native warriors' (11); the story offers a 'picture of the cruelty and fierceness of the savage warfare of those periods' (11). Cooper then describes the 'savage' violence which the Indians practised against the isolated white colonists:

> The terrific character of their merciless enemies, increased, immeasurably, the natural horrors of warfare. Numberless recent massacres were still vivid in [the colonists'] recollections; nor was there any ear . . . so deaf as not to have drunk in with avidity the narrative of some fearful tale of midnight murder, in which the natives of the forest were the principal and barbarous actors.(13)

Cooper's novel echoes the countless captivity narratives that formed a major sort of 'fearful tales' that the early American reading public 'drunk in with avidity'. These were usually atrocity stories, of course, illustrating why 'savagery' had to die out.[11] Cora and Alice must be twice rescued from captivity: the second time, Cora dies along with Uncas and Magua. As the French and British fade from view, moreover, the main scenes show Indians exterminating Indians, with much help from Natty's 'long carbeen'. In short, Cooper portrays the extinction of the Mohicans and, by analogy, all other Indians as auto-genocide.

In both his racist stereotyping and his sympathetic defences of the Indians, Natty gives voice to the 'Manichaean aesthetic' central not just to Cooper's fiction but also to the entire genre of captivity narratives, and beyond this genre to imperialist discourse in general (see JanMohammed, 1983). H. Rider Haggard's *King Solomon's Mines*, for example, is marked by the same contradiction: like Chingachgook, the noble savage Umslopagaas teams up with Allan Quatermain to do battle against the hordes of diabolical, cannibalistic savages they encounter. Except for the most blatantly racist versions, imperialist narratives usually offer depictions of 'the good native' – often 'noble savage' – who collaborates with the good white characters in stamping out 'savagery' and promoting 'civilization'. Such narratives also offer versions of Natty Bumppo or Allan Quatermain; that is, of the white hero who learns the ways of the savages so effectively that he can function simultaneously both as their greatest friend and as their deadliest exterminator.

This is not to say that such characters are merely imaginary: there were plenty of Natty Bumppos on the imperial frontiers everywhere in the world over the last five centuries – the bosom-buddies of Indians, Zulus or Maoris who were also ruthless killers of Indians, Zulus or Maoris. So it does not seem out of character when, during their first escape from captivity, Natty sounds like Conrad's Kurtz: 'Extarminate the varlets! no quarter to an accursed Mingo!' (112). At the end of the ensuing battle, the ground strewn with Mingo corpses, 'the honest, but implacable scout . . . made the circuit of the dead' and, to make sure they really are dead, 'into [their] senseless bosoms he thrust his long knife, with as much coolness as though they had been so many brute carcasses' (114). There is no telling how many Mingoes Natty shoots, stabs or bludgeons. But the massacring of Mingoes is apparently justified by the Mingoes' own bloodthirsty habits of capturing, torturing and massacring whites and, of course, good Indians like the Delawares.

Quite apart from the evil machinations of Magua, who lusts after Cora, the grisliest episode in the novel reveals a 'savagery' so ferocious as to demand its total extinction. When the British decamp from Fort William Henry, they are left by the French at the mercy of the Hurons. One Huron, attracted by a shawl in which a mother has wrapped her baby, snatches both away and, with 'a gleam of ferocity . . . dashed the head of the infant against a rock, and cast its quivering remains to her very feet' (175). When the mother falls on her knees to pray for deliverance, the Huron, 'maddened' because another has grabbed the shawl, 'and excited at the sight of blood . . . mercifully drove his tomahawk into her . . . brain' (175). There ensues a general massacre of the innocents by 'more than two thousand raving savages' (176), during which 'the flow of blood [became] a torrent; and as the natives became heated and maddened by the sight, many among them even kneeled to the earth, and drank freely, exultingly, hellishly, of the crimson tide' (176). This is the one instance in the story of cannibalism, which everywhere in imperialist discourse represents the absolute nadir of inhumanity – a sure sign that its practitioners are uncivilizable. The sentiment that such atrocities are meant to arouse is, of course, identical to Kurtz's at the end of his report on the suppression of savage customs: 'Exterminate all the brutes!'

Natty helps the cause of civilization – helps the white future to blossom in the howling wilderness – by fighting savagery with savagery, which might otherwise take too long to exterminate itself, so to speak. The slaying of Uncas by Magua is just the final touch, necessitating that the culturally half-savage Natty end the racial savagery by slaying Magua. That the slaughter is already part of history, located in the pre-revolutionary past, underscores the inevitability of the future extinction of all Indians. The Western, imperialist concept of 'savagery' is of course bound up with the past: like the 'last of the Mohicans', 'savagery' is lost to history, it has no future; the future everywhere belongs to 'civilization'. Cooper's ascription of the Indians to a futureless past is the sort of temporal displacement that Johannes Fabian calls the 'denial of coevalness' and that imperialist discourse practises upon all 'primitive' societies.[12] The illusion that certain peoples, races or cultures do not belong to the present is intrinsic to the word 'primitive', which of course means archaic – and therefore out of date, belated, passé. The primitive or savage whose time has come – or whose race's time has come – is *the* central figure of the Other in imperialist discourse, as in William Sharp's 1884 poem 'The Last Aboriginal'. Here, the last of his race is not a Mohican, but an Australian:

> I see him sit, wild-eyed, alone,
> Amidst gaunt, spectral, moonlit gums;
> He waits for death.

The phrase 'Stone Age savage' is another obvious example of the 'denial of coevalness' – a denial frequently figured by death, as in all predictions of the inevitable extinction of those 'primitive races' that prove unable to speak the present and future tenses of history by becoming civilized. Chingachgook mourns his son and his entire race; he can speak only in the sentimentalized past tense of elegy.

But 'denial of coevalness' can also paradoxically be figured by childhood, as when Cooper, Jackson and many others refer to Indians as 'the children of the forest'.[13] Lora Romero (1991: 392) notes that 'Cooper incorporates the racial other as an earlier and now irretrievably lost version of the self'.[14] Like Conrad's Marlow or Haggard's Quatermain, Cooper's pale-faces who venture into the 'wilderness' are venturing into areas heretofore bereft of both history and future, a space out of time. Cooper's Indians are, like Australian aborigines according to the recently rescinded legal doctrine of *terra nullius*, prehistoric inhabitants of otherwise empty land that belongs to nobody. Their prehistorical status is registered partly in their childishness; Chingachgook and Uncas are savage Peter Pans, 'children of the forest' who do not because they cannot grow up.

The metaphor of the savage as futureless child is related to discourse about economic development, based on the assumption that societies, like individuals, can grow up or mature. A famous example of the 'growing up' metaphor occurs in Kant's 1784 essay, 'Was ist Aufklärung?'. Kant's answer is that Enlightenment as both a historical process and a period – the period that inaugurates *modern* history – is the progress of society from immaturity to maturity. And maturity, Kant says, means the achievement of full Enlightenment, or of the full exercise of public, democratic and scientific reason for human betterment. A version of Kant's argument is inscribed today in development discourse, according to which societies that possess advanced economic and political capacities are said to be 'mature'; the so-called underdeveloped societies of the so-called Third World are said to be 'immature', like Cooper's 'childish' Indians. But as André Gunther Frank and other critics of the ideology of 'development' contend, it isn't the case that the supposed immaturity of, say, Iraq or Bosnia is just a natural stage through which those nation-states are inevitably passing on the progressive road to modern 'maturity'. Frank contends that the 'underdevelopment' of the so-called Third World is the result of the 'development' of the First World. In other words, the supposed 'maturation' or modernization of some nation-states occurs at the expense of the *imposed* 'immaturity' or perhaps even infantilization of others.[15]

But something worse than infantilization or imposed underdevelopment has been the fate of societies that have resisted the forces of 'development'. As Zygmunt Bauman (1989) contends, genocide and development have marched together through modern history. Of course, the ideology of economic modernization can be socialist or communist as well as bourgeois or capitalist, but in either case it is identified with the progress of civilization, and in either case societies that resist do so 'on pain of extinction' – the fate of perhaps 95 per cent of the original Native American population (Stannard, 1992: x).[16]

Cooper does not expect his Indians to develop or mature; he expects them to die. His 'children of the forest' are frozen in a pre-state immaturity, apparently without government and without law, as Thomas Jefferson for one declared them to be (Drinnon, 1980: 78–98). For Cooper, the metaphor of the savage as futureless child crystallizes in the death of the man-child Uncas, the last child and the last hope of the Mohicans. This metaphor is underscored by the final words of the novel, in which Natty comforts Chingachgook for the loss of his child, and hence the loss of the future of his race: 'I have no kin, and I may also say, like you, no people. He was your son, and a red-skin by nature . . . but if ever I forget the lad . . . may He who made us all, whatever may be our colour or our gifts, forget me!' (349). Here the story dissolves into philanthropic tears:

> Chingachgook grasped the hand that, in the warmth of feeling, the scout had stretched across the fresh earth, and in that attitude of friendship, these two sturdy and intrepid woodsmen bowed their heads together, while scalding tears fell to their feet, watering the grave of Uncas, like drops of rain. (349)

The movie botches this philanthropically tearful ending, as it botches almost everything else in the novel, by having Russell Means speak these incongruous last words: 'I, Chingachgook, last of the Mohicans. . . .' Of course, Chingachgook is literally the last of his race, but to identify him, rather than Uncas, as the final Mohican obliterates the racist metaphor at the heart of Cooper's fantasy – the metaphor of the savage as futureless child. After the first rescue of Cora and Alice from the evil Hurons, Uncas – futureless and last child of the childlike Mohicans – expresses an 'instinctive delicacy' and 'sympathy' that, the narrator says, 'elevated him far above the intelligence, and advanced him probably centuries before the practices of his nation' (115). So the last Mohican is also the best, the exemplar of a future civilization that his 'race', already extinct but for Uncas and Chingachgook, will never achieve. Racist though it is, the poignancy of this displacement in time, this loss of both history and future, is the central message of Cooper's elegy. The movie is unfaithful to the novel precisely because it erases Cooper's – and nineteenth-century America's – racist understanding of savagery.

This erasure is highly ironic, given Mann's 'obsession with even the smallest detail' regarding everything from 'the colors and patterns of each tribe's war paints' to finding 'the few remaining old-growth forests that most resembled the terrain Cooper wrote about' (Ansen, 1992: 49). Mann even 'insisted on building everything from the muskets to the fort from scratch, using original materials' (ibid.) But while Mann pursued historical *details* obsessively, he forgot the big picture – I mean the central message of Cooper's novel: its sentimental racism which, applied to savagery, equals elegy. Along with denial, forgetting or trivialization, sentimental racism is *the* main way that white America has interpreted its genocidal conflict with Native Americans, both then and now.

In a sense, however, the movie perfects Cooper's novel. The movie looks remorselessly, cynically upon the historical violence that it portrays – and yet it identifies nothing whatsoever racist about that violence. But the novel already looked remorselessly, cynically and with sentimental equanimity (these are indistinguishable terms) upon what Cooper saw as the inevitable extinction of all savagery by savagery – a sentimentalism all the more insidious because it obscures or fails to perceive its own racism. Identifying Chingachgook rather than Uncas as 'the last of the Mohicans' is paralleled in the movie by causing the blonde, blue-eyed Alice to die rather than the raven-haired Cora with her 'taint' of African blood. The film contains no hint of the 'tragic mulatta' motif. Perhaps it semi-compensates for its erasure of Cooper's racism by converting the ageing Natty Bumppo into the young, gorgeous Daniel Day-Lewis, who falls in love with the equally gorgeous albeit raven-haired Cora, played by Madeleine Stowe.

The movie is certainly sexier than the novel, but the film love affair between Natty and Cora also obliterates the erotic side of Cooper's story, which is specifically *both* interracial and racist: the attraction both Magua and Uncas feel towards Cora. When it comes to sex, Cooper's Natty Bumppo is even more childlike than the Indians. Whereas no hint of the amorous seems ever to enter the 'honest, but implacable' head of the ageing frontiersman, Cooper's Indians are creatures of emotion and often of 'unbridled passions'. Except for Magua's lust and one brief, ambiguous interlude between Uncas and the blonde, blue-eyed Alice, the movie de-sexes the Indians and offers up a thoroughly rejuvenated Natty Bumppo as sex symbol.

Like many recent film-makers, Mann seems to have been partly motivated by the philanthropic wish to portray Native Americans more sympathetically than earlier film-makers have done. Why else have Russell Means play Chingachgook? But if the undoing of Cooper's racism was part of Mann's purpose, he has undone it by erasing it. The result is the undoing of Cooper's racist novel, so perhaps a better name for the movie would have been *The Last of the Last of the Mohicans*. The forgetting of Cooper's racism by the movie is so total that the question of the final extinction, whether through genocide or auto-genocide, of the Mohicans and, beyond that, of all Indians, never comes into play, except in Russell Means's last words: 'I, Chingachgook, last of the Mohicans. . . .' By evading the central, energizing dynamic of Cooper's story – a racism that is both epic and elegiac – the movie fails to tell its viewers anything about the past. Instead it belongs to the now widely popular genre of nostalgic – or better, amnesiac – imperialist adventure tales like the Indiana Jones movies.

Just as the novel robs the Indians of history, the film practises the same sort of historical robbery on the novel. Contrary to what their makers may believe they are doing, such novels and films tend only to recycle the imperialist racism they might otherwise be anatomizing and resisting. Thus sadly, ironically, one thing hasn't changed in Michael Mann's film: as in Cooper's novel, a 'redskin' is a 'redskin', even when played by Russell Means. And thus sadly, ironically, one thing that hasn't changed in Washington, DC, home of the new United States Holocaust Museum but also both of the Bureau of Indian Affairs and of the Washington Redskins: 'redskins' who aren't pro athletes – Atlanta Braves, Cleveland Indians – do not count for much in the national scheme of things.[17] Perhaps therefore I should end with the semi-wise words of the old Sachem in Mann's remake (or travesty) of Cooper's novel – the only interesting language that I can detect in the film script: 'The white man came and night entered the future with him.'

Notes

1 In *Modernity and the Holocaust* (1989), Zygmunt Bauman argues that the Nazi Holocaust against the Jews, horrific as that recent historical nightmare was, was far from unique. Instead, modernity includes within its social conformation the ingredients for repeated holocausts. We forget these ingredients at our peril. If the history of the Americas cannot be written in terms of a single, condensed, deliberate genocide, then it needs to be understood as a series of genocides, especially against Native and African Americans. Indeed, the larger,

global history of European expansion and imperialism from the Renaissance or perhaps even the Crusades forward, needs to be understood in relation to the concept of genocide. On forgetting the Nazi Holocaust, besides Lyotard's *The Differend* (1988), see Pierre Vidal-Naquet, *Assassins of Memory*.

2 It may seem illogical to call slavery 'genocide', when it was in the slavers' and slave-owners' interests to keep slaves alive rather than to murder them, but millions of Africans lost their lives through disease or through the various forms of violence and horror that were visited upon them in bondage.

3 On the U.N. Convention on Genocide, see Churchill, *Indians Are Us?* (1994: 11–63).

4 See e.g. H. Daniel Peck (1988), who compares Cooper to more 'realistic' (that is, partly, less philanthropically sentimental) 'writers of the frontier' like Robert Montgomery Bird, whose *Nick of the Woods* (1837) depicts all Indians as diabolical savages deserving only to be slaughtered. In contrast to Bird, Peck's Cooper is an almost saintly early American mythologizer who faithfully records 'the tragedy' of the Indians' 'dispossession' (Peck does not use any stronger term like 'genocide'). At least Bird was honest about his race hatred. Cooper's sentimental racism, like President Jackson's 'Philanthropy' (see above), produces the mystification of genocide as auto-genocide – either hypocrisy or else a form of insidious, politically unconscious ideology.

5 At the end of Chapter 3, Natty announces that he is 'a man, who, his very enemies will own, has no cross in his blood' (35); later references to his being a 'man without a cross' refer back to this assertion about his racial purity. Earlier in the same chapter, Natty says to Chingachgook and Uncas: 'I am not a prejudiced man, nor one who vaunts himself on his natural privileges, though the worst enemy I have on earth, and he is an Iroquois, daren't deny that I am genuine white' (31).

6 For the concept of the 'Great Zero', see Lyotard, *Libidinal Economy* (1993: 1–13).

7 Compare *Notions of the Americans*, where Cooper writes: 'As a rule the red man disappears before the superior moral and physical influence of the White, just as I believe the black man will eventually do' (1991: 483).

8 Throughout imperialist discourse, there are numerous analogues to Cooper's and Irving's opinions about the self-extinguishing tendency of 'savagery'. For example, in her free-trade fantasy *Dawn Island*, written for the Anti-Corn Law League in 1845, Harriet Martineau describes a society where, before the coming of the British, the 'savages' are so very savage that they threaten their own extinction (Brantlinger, 1986: 30–2). The wisest among them, old Miava, foresees the time when 'man shall cease'. In a reversal of the Malthusian nightmare, constant warfare, cannibalism and infanticide will soon depopulate the island; fortunately the 'dawn' – the arrival of a British ship signalling the advent of commerce and civilization – saves the islanders from their collective suicide. But at least Martineau's 'Dawn Islanders' have a future – at least they can become civilized – which is more than can be said of Cooper's Mohicans, or of Cooper's and Irving's Indians in general. Martineau offers a paradigmatic

version of one of the most frequent rationalizations for the 'vanishing' or 'passing' – that is, the extinction – of non-Western peoples under the imperializing onslaught of so-called 'civilization'.

9 For Jackson, see Rogin (1975: 13), and also Stannard (1992: 121–4). By this comparison to Jackson, I don't quite mean to suggest that either Cooper or Natty Bumppo shares the widespread nineteenth-century view that the only good Indian is a dead one. In his recent essay collection *Crossbloods*, Gerald Vizenor offers several illustrations of this murderous sentiment: 'Who can forget the slaughter of tribal people at Mystic River, and Sand Creek, and Wounded Knee. . . . "We had sufficient light from the word of God for our proceedings," said John Underhill at Mystic River. "The only good Indians I ever saw were dead," said General . . . Sheridan at Fort Cob. "I have come to kill Indians, and believe it is right and honorable to use any means under God's heaven to kill Indians," said Colonel . . . Covington at Sand Creek' (1990: 165). But while the divinity of Indian killing isn't exactly a view that Natty Bumppo subscribes to – after all, he is the great friend of Chingachgook, Uncas, and all 'honest' Delaware Indians, at least – he entertains no qualms about slaughtering their Huron enemies.

10 Here is a sampling of the adjectives that both the narrator and Natty apply to the Hurons and to other non-Delaware Indians: merciless, treacherous, thievish, greedy, lying, malignant, fierce, cunning, gluttonous, vindictive, malicious. At times these ignoble qualities are attributed to *all* Indians, as when Natty says that 'revenge is an Indian feeling' (183), or when he speaks of 'Indian treachery' (52). Throughout, he refers to his 'redskin' enemies as demons or devils: they are 'imps', 'hell-hounds' (70), 'children of the devil' (76, 231), and 'malicious demons' (237). He often also calls them 'sarpents' or 'skulking reptyle[s]' bent upon 'deviltry' (202). This is true, even though the name of his bosom-buddy Chingachgook means 'big sarpent' (57), and even though, when the Bible-toting David Gamut says of Indians in general that 'they are among the profanest of the idolatrous' (226), Natty jumps to their defence: 'Therein you belie the nature of an Indian [says Natty]. Even the Mingo adores but the true and living God! 'Tis a wicked fabrication of the whites . . . that would make a warrior bow down before images of his own creation. It is true, they endeavour to make truces with the wicked one – as who would not with an enemy he cannot conquer! – but they look up for favor and assistance to the Great and Good Spirit only' (226).

11 Annette Kolodny (1993) points out that captivity narratives have been a staple of American culture down to our own time in both fiction and film, and also that they are more complicated and contradictory than is usually acknowledged. While they were often provocations to intervention and even to the extermination of 'the savages' who sometimes did capture whites, including white women and children, they sometimes also, by performing a sort of amateur ethnography, offer sympathetic accounts of Indian ways of life. Cooper's novel does both. On the one hand, it presents a sympathetic portrait of Natty Bumppo's favourite Indians, the 'honest'

Delawares and their 'noble' but vanishing offshoot, the Mohicans. On the other hand, it presents Magua and the thieving, diabolical Hurons in a lurid light every bit as stereotypic as anything to be found in the crudest captivity narratives.

12 'Primitive being essentially a temporal concept,' writes Fabian, it 'is a category, not an object, of Western thought' (1983: 18)

13 Writing in 1859, for instance, Horace Greeley declared that 'The Indians are children' (quoted in Rogin, 1975: 117).

14 'Going up that river was like travelling back to the earliest beginnings of the world', says Marlow in *Heart of Darkness* (34); both the landscape and the Congolese people seem to him 'prehistoric' – that is, they both have *no* history, which is what Hegel said about the entire continent of Africa, and they have *no* future, because they have already fallen out of history, they are prior to historical time itself. As Edward Said points out, the 'cartographic impulse' in imperialist discourse always maps the uncolonized spaces of the earth as 'wilderness' or 'desert', 'waste places' or 'areas of darkness' (Said, 1993: 226). An extreme example was the doctrine of *terra nullius* in Australian law, which asserted that, before the arrival of the First Fleet in 1788, Australia was empty land, belonging to nobody. This doctrine was part of Australian law until June 1992, when, in the Eddy Mabo land rights case, the High Court overturned it, thereby implying that the aborigines were, after all, somebody.

15 'Underdevelopment is not due to . . . archaic institutions and . . . capital shortage in regions that have remained isolated from the stream of world history,' writes Frank. 'On the contrary, underdevelopment was and still is generated by the very same historical process which also generated economic development: the development of capitalism itself' (Frank, 1967: 9); see also Amin (1977); Castoriadis (1991).

16 The phrase 'on pain of extinction' occurs in Marx and Engels, who wrote: 'by the rapid improvement of all instruments of production, by the immensely facilitated means of communication, [the bourgeoisie] draws all, even the most barbarian, nations into civilization. The cheap prices of its commodities are the heavy artillery with which it batters down all Chinese walls. . . . It compels all nations, *on pain of extinction*, to adopt the bourgeois mode of production' (477).

17 See Churchill, 'Crimes against humanity' (1993) on the Washington Redskins, the Atlanta Braves, the Kansas City Chiefs, the Cleveland Indians, and so on.

References

Amin, Samir (1977) *Imperialism and Unequal Development*, New York: Monthly Review Press.

Ansen, David (1992) 'Mann in the wilderness', *Newsweek*, 28 September: 48–9.

Bauman, Zygmunt (1989) *Modernity and the Holocaust*, Ithaca: Cornell University Press.

Brantlinger, Patrick (1986) *Rule of Darkness: British Literature and Imperialism, 1830–1914*. Ithaca: Cornell University Press.

Castoriadis, Cornelius (1991) 'Reflections on "rationality" and "development"', in *Philosophy, Politics, Autonomy: Essays in Political Philosophy*, Oxford: Oxford University Press.

Churchill, Ward (1993) 'Crimes against humanity', *Z Magazine*, March: 43–7.

—— (1994) *Indians Are Us? Culture and Genocide in Native North America*, Monroe, ME: Common Courage Press.

Conrad, Joseph (1963) *Heart of Darkness*, New York: Norton.

Cooper, James Fenimore (1990) *The Last of the Mohicans*, Oxford: Oxford World's Classics.

—— (1991) *Notions of the Americans: Picked up by a Travelling Bachelor*, Albany: SUNY Press.

Cornell, Stephen (1988) *The Return of the Native: American Indian Political Resurgence*, New York: Oxford University Press.

Drinnon, Richard (1980) *Facing West: The Metaphysics of Indian-Hating and Empire Building*, Minneapolis: University of Minnesota Press.

Elliott, J. H. (1993) 'The rediscovery of America', *New York Review of Books*, 24 June: 36–41.

Fabian, Johannes (1983) *Time and the Other: How Anthropology Makes Its Object*, New York: Columbia University Press.

Frank, André Gunder (1967) *Capitalism and Underdevelopment in Latin America*, New York: Monthly Review Press.

Irving, Washington (1976) *Astoria: or, Anecdotes of an Enterprize beyond the Rocky Mountains*, Boston: Twayne.

Jaimes, M. Annette (ed.) (1992) *The State of Native America: Genocide, Colonization, and Resistance*, Boston: South End Press.

JanMohamed, Abdul R. (1983) *Manichean Aesthetics: The Politics of Literature in Colonial Africa*, Amherst: University of Massachusetts Press.

Kolodny, Annette (1993) 'Among the Indians: the uses of captivity', *The New York Times Book Review*, 31 January: 1, 26–29.

Lyotard, Jean-François (1988) *The Differend: Phrases in Dispute*, Minneapolis: University of Minnesota Press.

—— (1993) *Libidinal Economy*, Bloomington: Indiana University Press.

Maddox, Lucy (1991) *Removals: Nineteenth-Century American Literature and the Politics of Indian Affairs*, New York and Oxford: Oxford University Press.

Martin, Calvin (ed.) (1987) *The American Indian and the Problem of History*, New York and Oxford: Oxford University Press.

Pearce, Roy Harvey (1965) *The Savages of America: A Study of the Indian and the Idea of Civilization*, Baltimore: Johns Hopkins University Press.

Peck, H. Daniel (1988) 'James Fenimore Cooper and the writers of the frontier', in Emory Elliott (ed.), in *The Columbia Literary History of the United States*, New York: Columbia University Press.

Rafferty, Terrence (1992) 'Brave acts', *The New Yorker*, 5 October: 160–2.

Rogin, Michael Paul (1975) *Fathers and Children: Andrew Jackson and the Subjugation of the American Indian*, New York: Knopf.

Romero, Lora (1991) 'Vanishing Americans: gender, empire, and new historicism', *American Literature*, 63(3): 385–404.

Said, Edward (1993) *Culture and Imperialism*, New York: Knopf.

Slotkin, Richard (1973) *Regeneration through Violence: The Mythology of the American Frontier, 1600–1860*, Middletown, CT: Wesleyan University Press.

Stannard, David E. (1992) *American Holocaust: Columbus and the New World*, New York: Oxford University Press.

Vidal-Naquet, Pierre (1992) *Assassins of Memory: Essays on the Denial of Holocaust*, New York: Columbia University Press.

Vizenor, Gerald (1990) *Crossbloods: Bone Courts, Bingo, and Other Reports*: University of Minnesota Press.

Woodward, Kenneth (1993) 'We are witnesses', *Newsweek*. 26 April: 48–51.

Jane Blocker

ANA MENDIETA AND THE POLITICS OF THE *VENUS NEGRA*

Abstract

The theorizations by some early feminists of the affiliation between Earth and woman, the 'archetype of the Great Goddess', and the 'universal female', are today regarded with embarrassment as essentializing, ultimately disempowering gestures. This article examines a 1981 project by Cuban-born artist Ana Mendieta for the feminist art journal *Heresies*. In this project she combines a photograph of one of her own earthworks with her translation of the nineteenth-century Cuban legend *The Venus Negra*. By investigating this legend in the context of nineteenth-century Cuban nationalism, and this earthwork in terms of twentieth-century US/Latino politics, this article argues that the Earth is not necessarily the essential category it appears to be. It claims that the discursive deployment of the Earth – the nation's primitive Other – subverts ideologies of the nation and contributes to its performative renegotiation. Further, it suggests that, in using this legend to disrupt the hegemonic construction of nation, both the legend's authors and its contemporary translator play with the performativity of both gender and race.

Keywords Feminism; art history; performance studies; Ana Mendieta; nationalism; Cuban folklore

Color is not zero meaning; it is excess meaning.[1]

(Julia Kristeva)

The nation is no longer the sign of modernity under which cultural differences are homogenized in the 'horizontal' view of society. The nation reveals, in its ambivalent and vacillating representation, the ethnography of its own historicity and opens up the possibility of other narratives of the people and their difference.[2]

(Homi Bhabha)

La Venus Negra, based on a Cuban legend.

Ana Mendieta. *Silueta Series.* 1980. Earth and gunpowder.

Ana Mendieta

Around 1817, when Spanish colonists first set foot on the *Cayo Loco*—a key off the South Coast of Cuba near the city of Cienfuegos—they found a sole inhabitant. She was a young Black woman, nude except for necklace and bracelets of seeds and seashells, and so lovely that "the most demanding artist would have considered her an example of perfect feminine beauty." She was a survivor of innumerable generations of the Siboney Indians, who had been extinguished by colonization. They called her the Black Venus.

At the sight of the Spaniards, she ran—from fear rather than modesty. They caught her and discovered she was mute. Living alone on the *Cayo Loco*, she was accompanied everywhere by a white dove and a blue heron. Spreading their wings, they would touch her mouth with their beaks, in silent caress.

When one of the colonists took her home with him, gave her food and clothing, he expected her to please him and to work for him in return. But taken from her island freedom, and unable to speak, she nestled in a corner, refusing to get up, work or eat. Finally, alarmed at the prospect of her death by starvation, they took her back to the *Cayo Loco* to live in freedom.

From time to time over the years, the citizens of Cienfuegos tried again to "civilize" the Black Venus. But each time her passive protests forced them to return her to the key, where she reigned in solitude with the blue heron and the white dove her only subjects.

The historian Pedro Modesto recalled that when he was a child, around 1876, an old Black woman, with hair like a huge white powder puff and naked except for a blue, red and white necklace, secretly entered his house. She refused clothing and was dressed only by physical force. She refused all the food offered her except for native products—yucca, bananas and sweet potatoes. The next morning she had disappeared, leaving the clothes behind. That was the last time she was seen.

Today the Black Venus has become a legendary symbol against slavery. She represents the affirmation of a free and natural being who refused to be colonized.

Cuban artist Ana Mendieta has been making earth-body sculptures since 1973. She exhibits at A.I.R. Gallery in NYC and received a Guggenheim Fellowship in 1980.

22

Figure 1 Ana Mendieta's project '*La Venus Negra*, based on a Cuban legend' (*Heresies*, 4 (1) (1981): 22). Reproduced courtesy of the Estate of Ana Mendieta and Galerie Lelong, New York.

Introduction

IN 1981, CUBAN-BORN PERFORMANCE and earthwork artist Ana Mendieta (1948–85) incorporated the Cuban legend of the *Venus Negra* or Black Venus into a project for the feminist art journal *Heresies*.[3] Along with her translation of the story, she included a photograph of one of her own works, a piece she had executed in Iowa a year earlier (Figure 1). This earthwork is fairly typical of the numerous others which Mendieta created during her career; in it she moulds the earth into an iconic female body and digs out an inner cavity, which she then fills with gunpowder and sets ablaze. This black-and-white photograph, like the hundreds of other photographs which Mendieta took, serves as the only record of the earthwork/performance. By combining this image with a 100-year-old Cuban legend, Mendieta produces a text of great complexity, which gathers together rich and troubling elements from history, colonialism, exile, travel and political struggle.

As with other works that Mendieta executed in her fifteen-year career, this one appears in a network of performances which contribute to the ideological production of gender, race, ethnicity and nationality. In these works Mendieta employs performative strategies on multiple levels. The greater part of her oeuvre can be labelled 'performance art', since its purpose is not the realization of discreet objects but the involvement of Mendieta's own body with the Earth. The *Heresies* piece is, in this sense, doubly performative since it involves an original set of actions out of doors with dirt and fire, and a second set of interactions involved in appropriating the image of the first performance for publication by a feminist collective. Finally, since this work relates dialogically to an ethnographic text, it may be considered to engage the discourse of performativity. Although all these elements are important, this article will focus on the discursive production of performance.

Mendieta's work was profoundly affected by anthropological stories, which she often retold to help make clear the values, meanings and practices necessary to the production of her art. Specifically, she maintained a strong interest in the 'primitive', which she viewed as both a primary and a subversive category. She read Mircea Eliade's theories on comparative religion in 'modern' and 'traditional' societies, case studies on African tribespeople by Henri Junod and Lucien Lévy-Bruhl, and African and Cuban folklore. However, it is not enough to say that, in her concern with and writings about 'primitive' cultures, Mendieta *uses* ethnography; rather I would suggest that she *does* ethnography, in a specifically performative sense, by adopting its narratives and participating in the negotiation of their meanings. It is helpful in this context to consider James Clifford's definition of ethnography, which he sees as 'a performance emplotted by powerful stories'. 'Embodied in written reports,' he adds, 'these stories simultaneously describe real cultural events and make additional, moral, ideological, and even cosmological statements.'[4] Mendieta, perhaps more than the ethnographers from whom she took her ideas of the primitive, seems to broaden this notion of performance, if for no other reason than that she was more consciously aware of it. In this sense, the legend of the *Venus Negra* is indeed a powerful story.

The meaning of the *Heresies* project's textual collage involves the strategic combination in 1981 of the photograph and the legend, which had both been created originally in other contexts. In order to approach the meanings of this project, this article will examine both the nineteenth-century context in which the legend was created and its later use by Mendieta. What I hope to demonstrate through this examination is that both nineteenth-century Cuban Creoles (who are the legend's authors) and Ana Mendieta (the legend's translator) costume themselves as the character of the *Venus Negra* in order to perform their own victimization. In the case of the Creoles, since they are neither female nor black, they must stretch the meanings of gender and race in order to position themselves as victims of Spanish domination, while simultaneously securing their hegemonic control of African slaves. In this costume they reject attempts by Spain to dictate the meaning and limits of their nation-space and the nature of their agricultural economy. To do this they liberate the body, race and nation from essentialist meanings, while at the same time appealing to an essentialist notion of the 'Earth' as a primary, unchanging, legitimizing category. Mendieta, I will argue, builds on this work by unfixing the meanings of colour and nation relative to twentieth-century US/Cuban politics and, like the Creoles, essentializing the category of the Earth. Finally, I will suggest that while similar strategies are involved in the performances of this legend, Mendieta's cannot be immediately disregarded as yet another example of a bankrupt essentialism, but essentialism itself must be seen as an empowering gesture in the context of her postcolonial politics. As Diana Fuss explains, 'when put into practice by the dispossessed themselves, essentialism can be powerfully displacing and disruptive.'[5]

The legend of the *Venus Negra*

Ostensibly, this is a story about a black female body, a troubling sign marked by gender and race difference. It is the story of a female Indian who resists enslavement, slips away, and haunts her potential captors. A vividly described character, the Black Venus requires a powerful image, one which is capable of suggesting her spectral nature, her potential subversion, her elusiveness. Mendieta painted an image in mud on a cave wall outside Havana in 1981 titled *The Venus Negra*, which seems at first to answer this description (Figure 2). This image, with its portrait-like orientation, attenuated limbs and earthen pigment, eerily pictures the Venus as spectre. However, Mendieta created this image only after she completed her project for *Heresies*, and only after she had combined the *Venus Negra* legend with an unrelated and, in some ways, irreconcilable image.

The image which Mendieta chose to include in this project is, unlike the mud

Figure 2 Ana Mendieta, Untitled (Silueta Series), 1980 (detail). Black-and-white photograph documenting gunpowder silueta executed outside Iowa City, Iowa. 400 3 530, edition of six. Reproduced courtesy of the Estate of Ana Mendieta and Galerie Lelong, New York.

painting, a thoroughly disappointing one (see Figure 1). Because of its awkward orientation (in which the ground is tipped up to meet the picture plane), it takes on an even more abstract quality than its painted counterpart. In addition, it depicts the anticlimax of an earthwork/performance (one that exists independently of this legend and seems to have little to do with it), so that the viewer is confronted only with its ashen remains. The image relates to but cannot contain this performance, the elements of which exceed its boundaries in time and space. This limitation encodes the image with its own inadequacy to contain the performativity of its constituent themes. Ironically, it is this very inadequacy which to some degree explains Mendieta's use of the image. Although seemingly unrelated diagetically to the *Venus Negra* legend, in its incompleteness and lack of distinct borders, this image parallels the legend's blurred history and narrative gaps. The photograph of the mud painting, on the other hand, forecloses such slippage by focusing on and making vivid the character and appearance of the Venus, and as a result capturing and controlling her. This is a story about a black female body and, like the *silueta* with which it appears, its efficacy is most keenly felt where it lets that body move.

Around 1817, when Spanish colonists first set foot on the Cayo Loco – a key off the South Coast of Cuba near the city of Cienfuegos – they found

> a sole inhabitant. She was a young Black woman nude except for necklace and bracelets of seeds and seashells, and so lovely that 'the most demanding artist would have considered her an example of perfect feminine beauty.' She was a survivor of innumerable generations of the Siboney Indians, who had been extinguished by colonization. They called her the Black Venus.
>
> At the sight of the Spaniards, she ran – from fear rather than modesty. They caught her and discovered she was mute. Living alone on the Cayo Loco, she was accompanied everywhere by a white dove and a blue heron. Spreading their wings, they would touch her mouth with their beaks in silent caress.
>
> When one of the colonists took her home with him, gave her food and clothing, he expected her to please him and to work for him in return. But taken from her island freedom, and unable to speak, she nestled in a corner, refusing to get up, work or eat. Finally, alarmed at the prospect of her death by starvation, they took her back to the Cayo Loco to live in freedom.
>
> From time to time over the years, the citizens of Cienfuegos tried again to 'civilize' the Black Venus. But each time her passive protests forced them to return her to the Key, where she reigned in solitude with the blue heron and the white dove her only subjects.
>
> The historian Pedro Modesto recalled that when he was a child, around 1876, an old Black woman, her hair like a huge white powder puff and naked except for a blue, red and white necklace, secretly entered his house. She refused clothing and was dressed only by physical force. She refused all food offered her except for native products – yucca, bananas and sweet potatoes. The next morning she had disappeared, leaving the clothes behind. That was the last time she was seen.
>
> Today the Black Venus has become a legendary symbol against slavery. She represents the affirmation of a free and natural being who refused to be colonized.[6]

In this fable, Cuban Creoles fantasize about a meeting in which Spanish colonists have one last glimpse of the Siboney Indians who had in reality long since vanished by 1817. By telling this story, the Creoles dissociate themselves from their Spanish ancestors and think romantically about the bravery of a race of people in whose genocide they are complicit.[7] Therefore the legend is only historical in the sense that it serves as a marker for a gap in the collective memory of the conquering race. The Venus is clearly a figment of the colonial imagination. An ambiguous historicity controls the power of her brazen black body.

One of the peculiarities of this tale is that, despite its status as legend, it employs the discourses of history and anthropology in order to signify the 'real'; its efficacy depends both on a rhetoric of fact and a discourse of origins. It seems on one level to be referring to a historical personage whose existence has been documented by scholars – Pedro Modesto – and whose appearance can be traced to a specific date – 1817 – and a real place – Cienfuegos. As much as this rhetorical strategy works to naturalize the story of the *Venus Negra*, there remains a profoundly fictional element that is at odds with the tale's production of a palpable reality, and which undermines its ostensible theme of Indian resistance. This element is most clear when the story is considered in light of other stories of colonization, which do not end so happily. One wonders in particular why, given the Spanish colonists' profound lack of squeamishness at the sight of other people's blood, they did not simply kill the *Venus Negra* rather than return her to her home. That she is spared suggests that the *Venus Negra* is always already a sign; she is not a person to get away or be killed, but a rare image. This is emphasized when we are told in the legend that she is so lovely that 'the most demanding artist would have considered her an example of perfect feminine beauty'. She is not only the Venus of Greek myth, but the Venus whose name sanctions an extensive history of European artistic production of the idealized nude. In order not to die she has to be extraordinarily beautiful; in order to be a sign her black body must be turned into a vision.

To what uses this vision has been put are of considerable importance to us here, for this is not really an anti-slavery success story. The fact is that this fable neither served a native identity nor the politics of insurgency among Indians. Rather, it provided a source for the formulation of nascent Creole-Cuban identity, an identity that had to be formed in contradistinction to that of the European Spanish during the nineteenth-century struggle for Cuban independence.[8] The story thus became a part of the nineteenth-century discourse promoting Cuban protest against the colonial domination of Spain.[9] Cuba was the last country in Latin America to be held by Spain. The successive uprisings, beginning in 1819 and occurring periodically until the Cuban War of Independence, came in response to stringent colonial policies and to Spain's mismanagement of Cuba's economic resources. Despite the great profits that their sugar and tobacco crops meant for the peninsular Spanish, Creoles were heavily taxed, but they could not occupy public posts, set up independent industries or have any rights to legal action against the Spaniards.[10] In this story, the white Creole clothes himself in the black female Indian body so as to perform the threat of victimization posed by the Spanish. But why this costume? Why has the Creole chosen the black female body as the vehicle for resistance, and what specifically are the goals which such a strategy might hope to achieve?

I want to demonstrate that this narrative is part of the performativity of the nation-space and that it is an attempt at reformulating the means by which the nation was imagined. It does this, I believe, by claiming a precolonial, prediscursive deed to the land that supercedes any claim by the Spanish. The story functions as what Homi Bhabha calls a 'counter-narrative of the nation', which disturbs 'those ideological manoeuvres through which "imagined communities" are given essentialist identities'.[11] In this counter-narrative an appeal is made to an essentialist notion of the land, as a more natural and primary category, in order to de-essentialize the nation, the Earth's secondary and culturally determined identity. The *Venus Negra* signifies the natural inhabitant of the island whose more legitimate claim to the land is threatened when she is unjustly captured by foreign colonists. As such, she rehearses the escape from foreign control that Cuban-Creoles would later enact in their revolution of 1898. Their right to self-determination is legitimized through a narrative strategy in which one essentialist category trumps another. The Creoles are the closest thing to 'natives' on the island, so their claim to its wealth of natural resources is stronger than that of the Spanish colonizers.

It is important to see that the happy ending which the legend promises is dependent, first, on the strict division between 'Earth' and 'nation', and second on the alignment of 'female' and 'black' with the 'Earth', all of which fall under the heading of the dispossessed. Through this narrative linkage the 'artificial internal coherence', to use Judith Butler's phrase, of gender and colour is disturbed so that white males can clothe themselves in a black female body. This 'drag' performance causes me to wonder, along with Butler, 'is drag the imitation of gender, or does it dramatize the signifying gestures through which gender itself is established?'[12] If the latter is the case then in choosing a black female as the incarnation of their own victimization, Creoles risk empowering the other (and arguably 'real') victims – women, blacks and Indians – in whose masks they perform their own independence. As a result, this narrative both deploys and attempts to control the subversive potential of gender and colour.[13]

Gender and the Earth

The value of the Black Venus costume is that when dressed in it one automatically moves closer to the Earth, to Nature itself. One becomes a native with a pre-ordained right to the land that was inconceivable in the period of exploration, but took on more rhetorical force in the nineteenth century when the original 'natives' had been largely eliminated and the stakes in claiming territory grew. That the Venus is aligned with the Earth is due in part to her gender; the long tradition associating the female body with the Earth culminates in sixteenth- and seventeenth-century representations of the 'New World' personified by the nude female body. In such representations the female body signifies both untouched beauty and sexual availability, both an admiration of nature and a desire to tame it in the service of expansionism. The kind of ambivalence that surrounds this traditional association finds its way into the legend of the *Venus Negra*.

The Venus is presented as though she were a naturalist's curio – the sole example of her kind. She is a rare and coveted specimen whose place in the explorer's notebook is secured by her gender and race difference, which defines

Figure 3 Ana Mendieta, Untitled (Venus Negra), 1980. Black-and-white photograph of mud-painted silueta executed in Cuba. Dimensions unknown. Reproduced courtesy of the Estate of Ana Mendieta and Galerie Lelong, New York.

her for the colonists as an object of loathing, as a sexually available object, and as a low-Other whose kinsmen were slain with trifling ease and little remorse. But at the same time she is a rare beauty to be admired, collected and preserved.[14] This ambivalent perception of the Indian body has an extensive pedigree stretching back to the time when Columbus first stepped on to the shores of this largest of the Caribbean islands. Columbus' diary is filled with careful notes on all strange new flora and fauna, in which are included representative examples of the Indians he meets.[15] The Indian woman inscribed there is like a beautiful parrot, a tall palm tree, an animal of unknown species, a beautiful, tropical, wild, primitive being of considerable interest to an explorer. But she is also simultaneously an object to be collected, used and destroyed. The travel accounts of early explorers are similarly replete with descriptions of the sexual use of the female Indian body, of frequent and brutal rapes that would never have been considered as such, and atrocious murders no more criminal than the hunting of wild animals.[16]

Within this tradition, the *Venus Negra* is a figure of huge ambivalence. She at once assumes a definitively 'low' position and a small measure of power, the only kind of power available to such a creature – her naturalness itself. By refusing to yield to the trappings of civilization she reclaims herself as untameable, and becomes that most noble of animals which one simply must return to the wild. Unlike so many of her kindred, she is not raped or murdered but returned to her home in what seems at first to be an unprecedented victory. However, she is no more free there than if she were on zoological display, for her life has been spared so that she can serve as the signifier of an ever-diminishing wilderness. She is a curiosity, the last of a species not far from extinction, and as such she symbolizes both the power of those who have accomplished this elimination and the nostalgic feelings about what has now been safely lost.

The Venus is quite literally associated with the land that she occupied, so much so that it is feared she will die if she is not returned to it. As a personification of the Earth, her acts of resistance may be characterized as a refusal to participate in an economy of agricultural exploitation. The refusal to eat anything 'except for native products – yucca, bananas and sweet potatoes' seems to be a reference to the particular history of Spanish exploitation of Cuban land. Cuba's ability to produce and trade in native products was destroyed by the planting of vast acres of sugar crops, which is not a native plant, and which brought neither food nor profit to native Cubans but to colonials back in Europe.[17] In addition, sugar and other colonial crops, which Eduardo Galeano (following José Martí) refers to as 'monocultures',[18] destroyed the ecological balance of the island, robbing the soil of essential nutrients, and placing the landscape at the mercy of the vagaries of the European markets.[19]

In light of the history of Cuban agrarian practice, the Venus' insistence on native foods seems in a larger sense to resist that aspect of colonization which is driven to exploit the land for profit. In this regard, the black body of the Venus takes on particular significance. The darkness of her skin becomes analogous to the darkness of the Earth; her body is a metaphor for the Cuban soil before colonization, a landscape that was still fed only by native plants. This part of the legend urges a return to native agricultural production, to self-determination among the Creole population. By their association with the *Venus Negra*, both the land and the Creoles are cast as victims of colonial intervention. This story depends on a rhetoric of 'first claims' to challenge the legitimacy of foreign control.

That she will not dress or work suggests that the *Venus Negra* will not engage in trade with the colonists. There is an expectation on the colonist's part that if he feeds and clothes her she will 'please him and . . . work for him in return'. He trades food and clothing and receives labour and sex in return. In this miniature economy the body of the Venus is the key to exchange; its clothing, nourishment, ability to labour and sexually satisfy are the coins of the colonial market. What secures the value of her body is primarily that it is female, but also that it is black. To the extent that the *Venus Negra* refuses to dress, her blatant blackness becomes an image of itself. In her refusal she tactically insists on her gender and colour difference; she insists on being Other. The colonists' attempts to clothe her are not driven so much by morality and shame as they are by the need to cover and neutralize her difference in a strategy of assimilation. The body of the *Venus Negra* is a constant reminder of what lies just beyond the parameters of 'civilization', just beyond the system of colonial control. Like some uncomfortable vestment, the Creoles wear their Spanish heritage and wait for a time when they can re-dress themselves in the costume of self-determination. Meanwhile, the *Venus Negra*'s body embodies blackness, proclaims colour, will not hide gender, and is a picture for desire and loathing.

Colour and the Earth

When Judith Butler writes that 'gender is performatively produced', she, like many other cultural theorists, liberates gender from its hegemonically constructed binarism.[20] While the legend of the *Venus Negra* and its use by Cuban-Creoles certainly demonstrates Butler's claim, I would like to add to it the possibility that colour is also 'performatively produced'. The verity of this idea may be seen most obviously in the notion of 'passing', in which one attempts to present oneself as a member of a race or group to which one does not customarily belong. While passing may not always refer to an actual physical passage or movement, I would like to consider it as such, to see it as a result of the performativity of colour, and in turn to see it as a site of subversion. In their use of the Black Venus legend to challenge the limits of their proscribed nation-space, in particular the Creoles seem to be critically and subversively 'passing' for black.

In order to view passing as a subversive performance in the specific context of this legend, I want to suggest the ways that I imagine colour is related to movement. First, it is through travel or exploration that groups take on colour; second, geographical regions are themselves associated with particular colours; and third, one's colour can change through travel from one location to another.

It is clear in this legend that the movements of Europeans to the Western hemisphere have literally produced an encounter with other colours, that the whiteness of the colonists only takes on a value as white in relation to those other colours against which it is viewed. The colonists stumble through the dense foliage of an undeveloped part of the island to discover the blackness of the *Venus Negra*. Indeed, in this story she *is* blackness itself, and although it is never explicitly stated, the colonists are white. Their travel from Europe to Cuba makes possible this encounter in which their own colour is defined against that of the native Indian. This process of colour definition hints at the real possibility of the Venus' subversiveness because, as Richard Dyer writes, the power of whiteness is secured by 'making it hard . . . to see whiteness'.[21] In this chance meeting in the forest, colour takes on a distinct clarity. The colonists become white in the presence of the Black Venus and their source of power is unmasked. The Creoles, whose pale skin might otherwise signify the ancestry they share with the colonists, dress up in a darker skin so as to be marked as the victims of colonial aggression.

Beyond the obvious fact that whites from Europe only *became* white when they encountered other races with distinctly different skin colours, there is another way in which we might say that colour is related to movement; that is, colour is often associated with geographical location. Tzvetan Todorov provides an example of this when he explains that in Columbus' need to find gold and other riches, he used both natural phenomena and native bodies as tools of divination. In Columbus' journals,

> blacks and parrots are . . . considered as the signs (the proofs) of heat, and heat as the sign of wealth. It is hardly surprising then that Columbus never fails to remark the abundance of parrots, the blackness of skins, and the intensity of the heat.[22]

In this example there is a conflation of natural, geographical phenomena and the colour of the inhabitants of a particular region. The Creoles appropriate this conflation to their own ends. They associate themselves with the specific geography of Cuba in order to claim natural ownership of it.

In addition to geography's relation to colour, land itself and one's associations with it seem to be implicated in colour definition. Here, the colour of the earth is aligned with the colour of those who work on it. For example, Eduardo Galeano describes the results of the fact that peasant farmers from a small village in Argentina have been forced to leave their farms for the chance of a better life in Buenos Aires:

> A few years ago sociologists asked the one hundred and fifty survivors of a La Rioja village if they saw any change in their former neighbors who had left and returned on visits. Those who had remained said enviously that yes, Buenos Aires had improved the emigrants' clothing, manners, and way of speaking. Some also found the emigrants to be 'whiter'.[23]

In this anecdote it becomes clear that dark skin is related to the countryside, farming and working with the soil, whereas light skin is associated with the city and all the 'civilization' it symbolizes. Moreover, this story indicates a third significant aspect of colour's performativity: colour becomes visible through travel, colour is related to particular types of geography, and most significantly, colour can change as a person moves closer to or further away from geographical locations like city and country. The implications of colour's instability are provocative, since it means that colour is an elusive category, that it can be used as a tool of social mobility. Through movement, colour achieves a liminal quality. Through its performativity one can pass – in both the sense of getting away with something and passing from one state of being to another. In this sense, Creoles pass for black in order to strengthen their associations with the earth, in this case meaning the land or soil of Cuba, which in turn allows them to legitimize their narrative of the nation-space and to challenge the story the Spanish have produced for them.

But this analysis comes nowhere near to exhausting the use of colour as a signifier in the story of the Black Venus. That she is black and not brown is another complex issue since black, although used to describe the native, must also refer to the African slave population in Cuba, which was at this time considerable. How can the Venus be black but not African? Why is she chosen as the one to get away, when the successful liberation of a black slave might represent the subversion of colonial authority with more urgency?

By 1817, Cuba had already been thoroughly colonized, and large cities had grown up around the island which were key centres for the transportation of goods from Mexico and South America to Europe. Interestingly, black slaves had been introduced to the island with the first conquistadors, and by the middle of the nineteenth century their population exceeded that of whites.[24] So what makes the encounter with another black body so significant? I believe it has to do on one level with the blatant nakedness of this body, and the rejection of European civilization that the refusal of clothes symbolizes. This black body, found in the remote countryside, wears instead the signs of its excess. It presumes to be natural, rural, uncivilized, the very colour of the earth. It is itself a sign of a crack in the colonial enterprise, a body and a region that have escaped 'civilization'.

On another level, however, the significance of this encounter with a black body results from the fact that it is not the same as the black bodies of the African slaves who had travelled to the colony from afar. Theirs is a blackness that signifies foreignness, hers is a blackness that signifies nativeness. In other words, her blackness marks her relationship with the earth, it allows her to claim an original deed to a very valuable plot of land. The blackness of the slaves allows them to claim nothing.

In addition, theirs is a blackness that was much more problematic in the context of the struggling colony. In very basic terms, although the Creole population was negotiating its independence from Spain, many Creoles feared severing all ties with Europe because they worried that without Spanish intervention there would be uncontrollable slave uprisings. Since their own prosperity (as a relative minority) depended on the brutal exploitation of blacks and mulattos (who were in the majority), it was of primary concern to maintain the machinations of slavery. They traded their independence for economic prosperity, while Spain persisted in stacking the deck in its own favour by continuing to import slaves illegally to the island, with the aim of outnumbering the white bodies with black ones.[25] In this situation the black African body served as a constant reminder of the Creoles' concession to Spain. 'In the face of every slave,' Robert Paquette writes, 'Creoles could see a mirror image of their own colonial servility.'[26]

It is clear then that the symbol of subversion of colonialism had to be carefully chosen; colour had to be black, but not *that* black. It had to be a blackness in which Creoles could feel pride and not fear, in which they could see themselves as powerful and not as just another kind of slave. Clothed in this particular shade – while dressed in a costume only tangentially resembling that of their most immediate victims – they could perform their own victimization. This shade had to be a blackness that no longer existed, a blackness that was more of history than of skin.

Ana Mendieta and the *Venus Negra*

I have already discussed to a certain extent the meanings this story was meant to have, the ways in which it suggests subversion while keeping it always under control. What I have hinted at, and what I would now like to discuss more directly, is the fact that I do see the *Venus Negra* as a subversive figure in that she utterly confounds the understanding of colour and gender. Despite their best intentions, the unknown authors of this story, in order to achieve certain national and colonial goals, have had to make essential categories slippery. Like the Black Venus, colour and gender have escaped from them.

By employing this narrative in her project, Mendieta exploits this slipperiness to produce a work of bewildering complexity in which the meanings of gender, race and nation are by turns fixed and disrupted, then imbricated to such an extent that it is difficult to discuss them as separate entities. She essentializes the categories 'woman', 'colour' and 'earth', and then through her earthworks 'dresses up' as the Black Venus to perform exile and thereby produce a counter-narrative of the nation. Her strategy, although persistently problematic, carries great rhetorical force.

In terms of gender, it might at first appear that Mendieta's persistent use of the Earth/female body theme (both in the legend and in the earthwork that accompanies it) is part of a now passé element of 1970s feminism in which the Earth is seen in relationship to so-called goddess culture or the universal female. The attempts by artists such as Judy Chicago and Mary Beth Edelson to produce female goddess imagery and the spate of books produced in the late 1960s and early 1970s on this subject testifies to its importance to early feminist thought.[27] Certainly, many critics who have discussed Mendieta's work have done so in the shadow of such texts and images. Gloria Orenstein, for example, included Mendieta in her 1978 article for *Heresies* in which she discussed the 'Great Goddess' in contemporary art. Her effusive language and appeals to feminine spirituality seem troubling in retrospect:

> [Mendieta's] art concretizes that process of Earth Alchemy, using prime matter itself as the alchemistic vessel through which spirit will be made to

> reenter matter and transform woman into the vital incarnation of the Earth Goddess once more.[28]

Cast in these terms, Mendieta's earthwork (in which the earth is carved into a female body) becomes an embarrassing essentializing gesture that reinscribes patriarchal conceptions of the female while pretending to liberate woman through some vague conception of universal power, or, to quote another critic, 'the most basic aspects of femaleness'.[29]

Mendieta's use of the Black Venus legend does rely on an essentialist understanding of gender and colour. For Mendieta, the Black Venus stands for a kind of primitivism to which she herself felt a kinship. She writes tellingly on this subject that:

> It was perhaps during my childhood in Cuba that I first became fascinated by primitive art and cultures. It seems as if these cultures are provided with an inner knowledge, a closeness to natural resources. And it is this knowledge which gives reality to the images they have created.[30]

Here Mendieta herself seems to betray, in language only slightly different from that of the Spanish conquistadors, a belief that I have already discussed – the allegorical relationship between the darkness of the earth and the darkness of the skin. By appealing to this trope Mendieta risks producing a rhetoric informed by a tone of condescension and nostalgia of which anthropologists, like colonialists, have been all too guilty. However, her problematic use of this story is made more complex by and in response to feminism.

On one hand Mendieta pursues a strategy common to feminists of the late 1970s and early 1980s; that is, she attempts to see change in the future by searching for origins in the past that demonstrate the possibilities for women to break out of their prescribed roles. Through a strategy of passive resistance the *Venus Negra* challenges her male captors and wins her freedom. This emancipation rehearses the liberation of women that feminism attempts to enact. In short, Mendieta uses anthropological methods to define alternatives to the condition of women in her own time. But this rationale does not entirely resolve the troubling aspects of her strategy. It casts the Venus in two roles; she plays both a real Siboney Indian and Ana Mendieta herself, as Michelle Rosaldo has so insightfully explained.

> By using anthropology as precedent for modern arguments and claims, the 'primitive' emerges in accounts like these as the bearer of primordial human need. Women elsewhere are, it seems, the image of ourselves undressed, and the historical specificity of their lives and of our own becomes obscured. Their strengths prove that we can be strong.[31]

It therefore seems problematic for Mendieta to identify herself with the Siboney Indians, who exist only in legend and cannot speak for themselves. The mute

Venus in Mendieta's recasting of this tale is an apt symbol of the voiceless object of the ethnographic gaze. Unable to speak, the Venus cannot articulate her race difference and is thus in danger of having it effaced. In her need to find a precedent for female defiance to masculine power, Mendieta has overlooked an important problematic, as if she has forgotten that while she and the Venus share in gender, they do not share in colour.

On the other hand, this seemingly problematic strategy becomes less so when it is engaged as a critique of feminism's racial bias. Despite her decidedly white European heritage, as an artist in the United States Mendieta was not white; indeed, she was consigned to that amorphous realm of the non-white. This realm is ill-defined because in the US we have no room for the epistemological complexities of colour and race in Latin America (or anywhere else for that matter), and as a result we tend to describe people of widely divergent national, ethnic and racial backgrounds with radical imprecision.[32]

Since she is white *and* Cuban, a US citizen *and* an exile from a Third World country, Mendieta has neither a clearly defined colour nor a clearly enunciated nationhood. The sense of disempowerment attached to the ambiguity of this position prompted her to write in her Introduction to a 1980 exhibition of Third World women artists:

> During the mid to late sixties as women in the United States politicized themselves and came together in the Feminist Movement with the purpose to end the domination and exploitation by the white male culture, they failed to remember us. American Feminism as it stands is basically a white middle class movement. As non-white women our struggles are two-fold. This exhibition points not necessarily to the injustice or incapacity of a society that has not been willing to include us, but more towards a personal will to continue being 'other'.[33]

In this last statement, Mendieta invokes a stance remarkably similar to the one taken by the *Venus Negra*, who also seems driven by a 'personal will to continue being "other"'. She does not express a desire for inclusion, which would mean racial and cultural assimilation, but for difference. She affirms instead the performative power of exile. It would appear that Mendieta performed this exilic identity by embracing the colour which racism had assigned to her. Instead of passing for white, Mendieta was passing for black, a blackness that she understood through her own experience to be elusive, marginal and uncontainable.

Roberto Fernández Retamar explains the impetus for Cubans of white European ancestry to align themselves with native Indians and slaves, in a sense, to become black. The epithet *mambí*, Retamar writes,

> was disparagingly imposed on us by our enemies at the time of the war of independence. . . . To offend us they call us *mambí*, they call us *black*; but

> we reclaim as a mark of glory the honor of considering ourselves descendants of the *mambí*, descendants of the rebel, runaway, *independentista*, black – *never* descendants of the slave holder.[34]

This mutability of colour is essential to what the Cuban writer José Martí would call 'our mestizo America',[35] an America in which identities are marked by hybridity.[36] Martí makes it clear, however, that 'mestizo' does not mean solely a mixture of blood, a child born of parents of different races, but also the irrevocable mixture of cultures that lies at the heart of Latin American history. Mestizo is as much a historical quality as a biological one. In addition to skin colour it suggests race, ethnicity, heritage and class and thereby proves not the possibility of naming colour, but its impossibility. Therefore, Mendieta's choice to associate herself with the *Venus Negra*, with the native Indian, is more complex than simply a consequence of a politics of liberal guilt, or a zealous desire to display some innate qualities of femaleness. It insists instead upon the liminal nature of colour, a purposeful confusing and mixing of the iconography inherent in the skin. It questions what colour is, how it relates to race, how it signifies in a cultural economy of privilege and exploitation.

Just as Cuban-Creoles essentialized the notion of earth in relation to their island, giving it a primary signification that deconstructs the imagined nation, so Mendieta employs an essentialized notion of the earth to problematize the meanings of the nation in her own era. There is a significant distinction between these deployments of the category 'earth', however. The Creoles' notion of earth relates to the soil or land of their country. It is thus coterminous with the island's borders. Mendieta's notion of earth is *the* Earth, an earth that is coterminous with the globe and therefore one that exceeds all national boundaries.

In expanding the horizons of her referent, Mendieta engages the politics of colour, gender, nation and race with issues of broad-scale environmentalism. Mendieta's *Heresies* project is included in an issue on ecology, the theme of which may be summarized by another contributor:

> Nature feminists repeatedly remind us that we are part of the earth and the universe, part of a great interdependent community of both animate and inanimate beings.[37]

The trope of the 'great interdependent community' to which the ecology movement must constantly refer is problematic for the narrative of nation, which depends, according to Homi Bhabha, on ideas of 'progress, homogeneity, cultural organicism' and deep national history.[38] In these terms, the notion of the Earth depends on both our ability to imagine its singularity of meaning and our ability to see it in contrast to the divisive multiplicity of nations.

The Earth, bounded only by its astronomical proportions, exposes the contentious, shifting, imaginary boundaries of the nations that attempt to divide it.

Mendieta's performance, in which the Earth burns with volcanic power, and her photographic remnant, in which there is no longer room to see a horizon, reveal the rhetorical power of such a global focus. As a result, this *silueta* is a potent image for those who are victimized by the ideology of the nation-space. Mendieta's project not only imbricates the female body with the land, not only troubles national boundaries with an appeal to the unboundedness of the Earth, but also sets essential categories into motion.

Notes

1 Julia Kristeva, 'Giotto's Joy', *Desire in Language* (New York: Columbia University Press, 1980), p. 221. While I am fond of this quotation and its implications for the discussion of race, I should make it clear that Kristeva is discussing the implications of colour in art, specifically Giotto's use of colour in the Arena Chapel.

2 Homi Bhabha (ed.) *Nation and Narration* (London: Routledge, 1990), p. 300.

3 Ana Mendieta was born in Havana, Cuba on 18 November 1948. In September 1961 she and her sister were sent to the United States as a result of the expansion of Fidel Castro's plans for the socialization of Cuba and the intensification of US/Cuban political conflict in the wake of the Bay of Pigs invasion. Mendieta and her sister were sent to an orphanage in Dubuque, Iowa, and then to a series of foster homes. They did not see their mother and their younger brother Ignacio until January 1966, when they too fled Cuba for the US. Their father, who had been imprisoned by the Castro regime for his links with the CIA, and the assistance he had provided in their failed invasion, finally joined the rest of his family in Cedar Rapids, Iowa in April 1979, some eighteen years since he had last seen his daughters.

Calling itself 'a feminist publication on art and politics', *Heresies*' first issue came out in January 1977, becoming another in a series of art publications, inspired by second-wave feminism, to engage gender issues.

4 James Clifford, 'On ethnographic allegory', in James Clifford and George E. Marcus (eds) *Writing Culture: The Poetics and Politics of Ethnography* (Berkeley: University of California Press, 1986), p. 98.

5 Diana Fuss, *Essentially Speaking: Feminism, Nature and Difference* (New York: Routledge, 1989), p. 32.

6 Ana Mendieta, 'La Venus Negra, based on a Cuban legend', *Heresies*, 4(1) (1981): 22. I suspect that Mendieta has taken this almost verbatim from Samuel Feijóo, *Mitos y leyendas en las villas* (Havana: Universidad Central de las Villas, 1965), pp. 61–4. Feijóo must in turn have taken it from Adrian del Valle's *Tradiciones y leyendas de Cienfuegos* (La Habana: Sociedad Editorial Cuba Contemporánea, 1919), pp. 117–24.

7 Before they knew what was happening, the Spaniards had so totally annihilated the Siboney that an archaeological investigation of their culture in 1941 would

only turn up a few shells and bones. See Cornelius Osgood, 'The Ciboney culture of Cayo Redondo, Cuba', *Yale Publications in Anthropology*, nos 25–6 (New Haven: Yale University Press, 1942), pp. 5–71.

8 See Jaime Suchlicki, *Cuba From Columbus to Castro* (Washington: Brassey's (US), Inc, 1990), pp. 53–8.

9 Robert L. Paquette, *Sugar is Made With Blood: The Conspiracy of La Escalera and the Conflict Between Empires Over Slavery in Cuba* (Middletown, CT: Wesleyan University Press, 1988), p. 258. Here Paquette refers to the Cuban literary movement known as 'siboneyisme' whose leader was Gabriel de la Concepción Valdés, known as Plácido. Paquette writes that the movement 'took hold among Plácido's young, educated white countrymen and . . . served by its selection and romanticization of Indian themes to attack Spanish rule and to inspire anticolonial thinking and indigenous nationalism' (p. 258).

10 Suchlicki, p. 57.

11 Bhabha, p. 300.

12 Judith Butler, *Gender Trouble: Feminism and the Subversion of Identity* (New York: Routledge, 1990), p. viii.

13 I don't want to overstate the possibility for empowerment of these subaltern groups. The threat posed by performing the liminality of race and gender is what Victor Turner calls a 'subversive flicker'. He writes: 'it is put into the service of normativeness almost as soon as it appears. Yet I see it as a kind of institutional capsule or pocket which contains the germ of future social developments' (*From Ritual To Theatre: The Human Seriousness of Play*, New York: PAJ Publications, 1982, p. 44).

14 For more on the sexual implications of the black female body and the ambivalent feelings about it, see Sander Gilman, 'The Hottentot and the prostitute: toward an iconography of female sexuality', *Difference and Pathology: Stereotypes of Sexuality, Race, and Madness* (Ithaca: Cornell University Press, 1985).

15 Tzvetan Todorov, *The Conquest of America: The Question of the Other*, trans. Richard Howard (New York: Harper & Row, 1984), p. 48.

16 Todorov, p. 49. See also Bartolomé de las Casas, *Brevissima relacion de la destruycion de los Indios* (Seville, 1552).

17 Eduardo Galeano, *Open Veins of Latin America: Five Centuries of the Pillage of a Continent*, trans. Cedric Belfrage (New York: Monthly Review Press, 1973), pp. 79–83.

18 Galeano, p. 75.

19 Ibid., p. 80.

20 Butler, p. 24.

21 Richard Dyer, 'White', *Screen*, 29(24) (Autumn 1988): 46.

22 Todorov, p. 21.

23 Galeano, p. 206.

24 Suchlicki, p. 30. Accurate figures to demonstrate this are hard to find, since it was in Cuba's interest to hide the numbers of Africans who were being brought to the island after slavery was abolished in 1879. According to Verena Martinez-Alier, in her book *Marriage, Class and Colour in Nineteenth Century*

Cuba, in 1846 there were 472,985 blacks and mulattos and 425,767 whites (Cambridge: Cambridge University Press, 1974), p. 3.

25 Paquette, p. 92.

26 Ibid., p. 87.

27 I am thinking here of such texts as Mary Daly's *Beyond God the Father* (1973), J. J. Bachofen's *Myth, Religion and Mother Right* (1967), Robert Graves' *The White Goddess* (1966), and Merlin Stone's *When God Was A Woman* (1978).

28 Gloria Orenstein, 'The reemergence of the archetype of the Great Goddess in art by contemporary women', *Heresies* (Spring 1978): 78.

29 Ellen Lubell, 'Ana Mendieta at Yvonne Seguy', *Art in America*, 71(6) (summer 1983): 161.

30 Ana Mendieta, in Robyn Brentano and Mark Savitt (eds) *112 Workshop/112 Greene Street: History Artists and Artworks* (New York: New York University Press, 1981), p. 278.

31 Michelle Rosaldo, 'The use and abuse of anthropology: reflections on feminism and cross-cultural understanding', *Signs*, 5(3) (spring 1980): 392.

32 The US has long used the rule of 'hypo-descent' to distinguish among races. This rule suggests that blackness is defined by blood, so that one drop of black blood makes a person black. Thus the distinction is seemingly made clear: there are only two colours, white and black, and they have little or nothing to do with appearance. This kind of distinction facilitates segregation: if there is not a spectrum of colours to contend with, but only two, segregation is a simple matter. For more on this, see Carlos Moore, 'Congo or Carabalí? Race relations in socialist Cuba,' *Caribbean Review*, XV(2) (Spring 1986): 12–15, 43; and Charles Wagley, 'On the concept of social race in the Americas', *Contemporary Cultures and Societies of Latin America: A Reader in the Social Anthropology of Middle and South America and the Caribbean*, Dwight B. Heath and Richard N. Abrams (eds) (New York: Random House, 1965), pp. 531–44; and David Booth, 'Cuba, color and the Revolution', *Science and Society* XL(2) (summer 1976): 129–72.

33 Ana Mendieta, *Dialectics of Isolation: An Exhibition of Third World Women Artists of the United States* (New York: AIR Gallery, 1980), unpaginated.

34 Roberto Fernández Retamar, *Caliban and Other Essays*, trans. Edward Baker (Minneapolis: University of Minnesota Press, 1989), p. 16.

35 José Martí, *En Los Estados Unidos* (Madrid: El Libro de Bolsillo Aliaza Editorial, 1968), p. 304.

36 It is important to keep in mind that when Martí uses the word 'America' he is referring to the Americas and specifically what we would call 'Latin America'. However, since 'America' is so often read as synonymous with the United States, I have chosen to use the designation 'Latin America' to avoid confusion.

37 Joan Griscom, 'On healing the nature/history split in feminist thought', *Heresies*, 4(1) (1981): 7.

38 Bhabha, p. 4.

Carol Mavor

ODOR DI FEMINA: THOUGH YOU MAY NOT SEE HER, YOU CAN CERTAINLY SMELL HER

Abstract

'Odor di Femina: Though you may not see her, you can certainly smell her', articulates the primacy of visualism in the history of psychoanalysis. In the first half of the study Mavor reveals how both the photographs of mentally ill women made under the direction of Freud's teacher Jean-Martin Charcot and the use of the visualist rhetoric in the writings of Charcot and Freud were regarded as proof of an always already diagnosed and conceptualized vision of sexual difference. Charcot's and most emphatically Freud's conception of the senses conventionally marked vision as masculine and the others (touch, hearing and especially smell) as feminine. Mavor then turns to Lacan to undo this historically gendered, power-hungry split between sight and the othered senses through his theory of the gaze as *objet petit a*, which reticulates the gaze and its conventional singular authority. Taking a cue from Lacan's provocative claim that 'a wild odour emanates' from the 'function of seeingness', Mavor pushes Lacan's theory of the gaze (which, she argues, has often been sorely misrepresented in feminist film theory and art history) towards an expanded constellation of the senses. Her excavation of Lacan loosens the gaze's hold on the site of seer/seen, subject/object and, especially, sight/smell. As a result, sight loses its historical pride of place among the senses.

Keywords Freud; Charcot; psychoanalysis; Lacan; smell; visualism; fetish; femininity

Long afterward, Oedipus, old and blinded, walked the roads. *He smelled a familiar smell*. It was the Sphinx. Oedipus said, 'I want to ask one question. Why didn't I recognize my mother?' 'You gave the wrong answer,' said the Sphinx. 'But that was what made everything possible,' said Oedipus. 'No,' she said. 'When I asked, What walks on four legs in the morning, two at

> noon, and three in the evening, you answered, Man. You didn't say anything about woman.' 'When you say Man,' said Oedipus, 'you include women too. Everyone knows that,' She said, 'That's what you think.'[1]

'A WILD ODOUR EMANATES' from the 'function of *seeingness* (*voyure*)': so says Jacques Lacan in *The Four Fundamental Concepts of Psycho-analysis*.[2] Taking a cue from Lacan's provocative claim, this text seeks to unearth Lacan's conceptualization of the gaze as an expanded constellation of the senses, in which sight loses its pride, its authority and its maleness. My goal is to excavate Lacan's notion of the gaze in order to loosen the gaze's hold on the site of seer/seen, subject/object and, especially, sight/smell: a smell rank with heterosexual presumption. In the words of Peggy Phelan:

> One term of the binary is marked with value, the other is unmarked. The male is marked with value; the female is unmarked, lacking measured value and meaning. Within this psycho-philosophical frame, cultural reproduction takes she who is unmarked and re-marks her, rhetorically and imagistically, while he who is marked with value is left unre-marked, in discursive paradigms and visual fields. He is the norm and therefore unremarkable; as the Other, it is she whom he marks.[3]

In other words: I value the unmarked (that which 'resists vision and may not be "really there" at all').[4] I take pleasure and sense Hope (who remained hidden under the lid of Pandora's box) in the rustle of leaves and language (*le bruissement de la langue*).[5] My middle finger slowly opens Pandora's ivory box and I am overcome with the strange *odor di femina*. I let the lid drop (I love the sound of its lid, a camera's slow shutter click in the absence of light). Eyes closed, I open it again; I finger its walls of silk, fur, desire.

In the first half of this article, I historicize a psychoanalytic conception of the senses, which conventionally marks vision as masculine and the other senses (touch, hearing and especially smell) as feminine. In the second half, I want to undo this historically gendered, power-hungry split between sight and the other(ed) senses through Lacan's theory of the gaze as *objet petit a*, a theory I find surprisingly sensate, reticulated and provocatively lacking in authority. I twist the skin of Lacan to find something more than a gaze, something zesty (maybe even pungent), a different gaze that enriches bodily relations, that refuses to let 'the look' dominate.

Seeing with Freud

> I should explain the camera obscura now before I go much further. If you're going to understand the stories that follow then you've got to have a clear

> working picture of the machine. Looking at the building you'd never guess what lay inside. The cold, beige painted concrete and the box-like architecture suggest little more than a storage shed or utility space. The only clues are the black letters, GIANT CAMERA, painted on the east wall.
>
> In those words lie the key to understanding the machine, for when you pass into the small dark chamber you have entered the insides of a camera, *a camera in which you are the film, or more precisely your memory is.*[6]

Freud developed his important theories of sexuality and the unconscious around *visual representations*. For example, Freud *imaged* the unconscious as an invisible receptacle of filmic and still screen memories that selectively play themselves out as signs.[7] Impressions are made even before the child's 'psychical apparatus' is 'completely receptive' and like 'a photographic exposure . . . can be developed after any interval of time and transformed into a picture.'[8] Similarly, in his 'A note upon the "mystic writing pad"', Freud images the unconscious as a waxen, magic writing tablet (a *Wunderblock*) that retains memories/pictures/marks from the past, even though they are not always readily accessible.[9] The experiences/images are consciously forgotten (apparently wiped clean), as if the cover-sheet of the *Wunderblock* had been lifted.

> But though they are no longer available to view, the lines that have been pressed onto it are in fact retained by the waxen support, where they form a permanent network of traces. And this Freud analogizes to the mental operations of memory and thus to the part of his topological model given over to the unconscious.[10]

Here it is not only the content of the inscriptions that takes weight, but also the *Wunderblock* as an object of visual attention, a surface to be looked at ('I have a disease,' writes Barthes, 'I *see* language'[11]), where text (and images) become pictured and (almost) vanish . . . white writing.[12] Likewise, Freud's recasting of the Oedipal myth as the entry into adult sexual life falls on the problem of seeing. Or rather, on the problem of seeing nothing (the mother without a penis). This, in turn, calls for a stopping of the look retrospectively, by re-fixing the gaze on an object that was on or near the mother before the horrifying primal glance. The (fetishized) object then stands in for the missing penis. This action of seeing and not seeing simultaneously (which makes a so-called absence into a presence) stands at the centre of the fetishizing gaze. 'It is,' as Emily Apter writes, 'a "not looking" sustained paradoxically through visual fixation on the substitute phallus.'[13]

The overriding sense and even documentation of fetishism as both male and visual is at the centre of Freudian psychoanalytic theory. As Apter has pointed out, 'despite his [Freud's] admission at the Vienna Psychoanalytic Society in 1909 that "all women . . . are clothing fetishists"', Freud typically supplied a male agent to the perversion by associating it with male homosexuality and (as we shall see) *feminized* coprophilic pleasure.[14]

Apter's essay 'Splitting hairs: female fetishism and postpartum sentimentality in Maupassant's fiction' (from her remarkable book, *Feminizing the Fetish: Psychoanalysis and Narrative Obsession in Turn-of-the-Century France*) undoes the gendered-biased reading of fetishism, by discovering fetish objects of women spilling out of the drawers of not only turn-of-the-century French literature (Guy de Maupassant), but also in the cabinets of French psychiatry (Gaëtan Gatian de Clérembault) or the cupboards of feminist art (Mary Kelly). While sniffing out traces of female fetishism, Apter comes across special boxes and bureaux and albums and other private places enshrouded with veils and fabrics and fur – all belonging to women – whose sole purpose is to preserve the relics of departed loved ones. The stories of loss range from spoiled love to death to merely growing up. Inside these feminine spaces we find letters, pressed flowers, locks of hair, nail clippings, pieces of clothing. Apter points out that this 'bric-a-brac-cluttered world' has been largely overlooked, even when it reaches a space of 'manic collectomania' because it has been naturalized as part of feminine culture.[15] Clérembault (Lacan's notorious teacher who shot himself in the mouth in front of a mirror) is of obvious interest to Apter because he is 'the first theorist of female fetishism'.[16] 'Fixated on cloth textures and draped fabric, he wrote on Greek costume and photographed Moroccan woman mysteriously enshrouded in their chadors and veils. Clérembault also diagnosed this same *passion des étoffes* in his female patients.'[17] (The latter has provoked the interest of Leslie Camhi, who has specifically written on Clérembault's analysis of hysterical, female, department store kleptomaniacs who 'derived intense sexual arousal and satisfaction from stealing silk, which they would fondle and rub against their bodies'.[18] Likewise, Apter reads the work of the contemporary American artist Mary Kelly (who collected and framed, among other things, her son's soiled nappy liners, fragments of his baby blanket and little cotton T-shirts) as 'ironically aestheticizing the negative associations surrounding [a mother's] rituals of melancholia . . . [by transforming] the maternal reliquary into a feminized poetics of mnemonic traces, constitutive in turn of a (now positively valorized) genre of sentimentality' (Figure 1).[19]

In 'Splitting hairs', Apter's examples of female fetishes are often visual, sometimes olfactory. Most, however, feel haptic, fixated as they so often are on the textures of hair, cloth, jewelry. Apter's story suggests that tactile stimulation has been used (especially in Clérembault's psychoanalytic work and Maupassant's fiction) to separate the girls from the boys; this is not unlike Freud's computation of smell with the feminine. It is as if women are to be seen . . . not seeing.

Not surprisingly, Freud characterized his own teacher Jean-Martin Charcot, the father of hysteria, as a 'seer'. In an obituary for Charcot, Freud wrote that he had 'an artistically gifted temperament – as he said himself he was a *visuel*, a

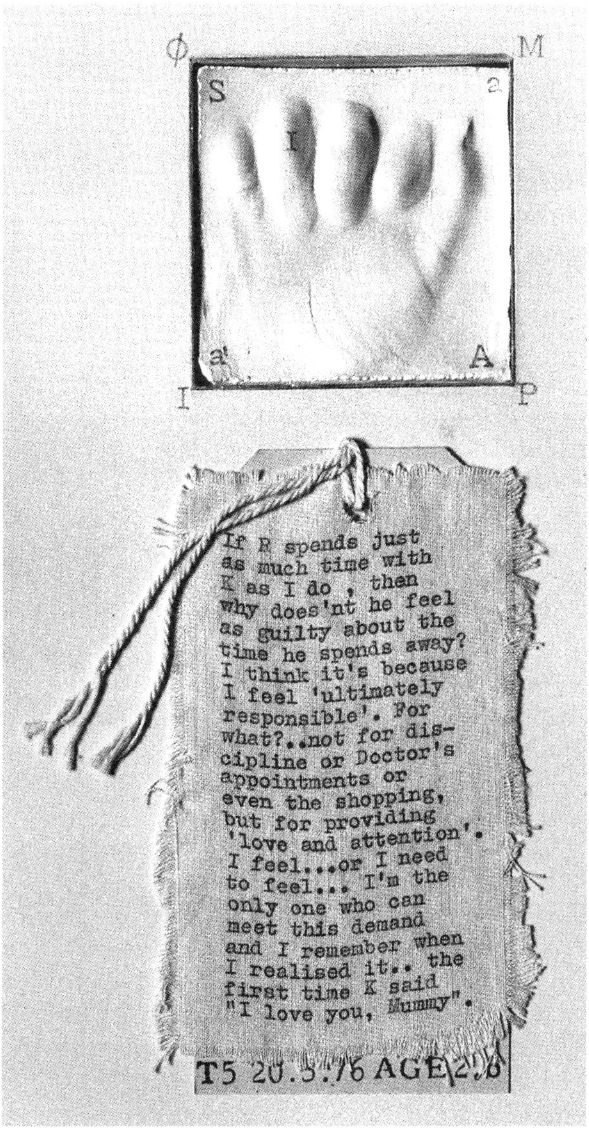

Figure 1 Mary Kelly, object from *Post-Partum Document*, 1976 'blankie' (the child's transitional object), plaster hand plaque (part of the mother's memorabilia, reminiscent of baby's first photos, shoes, locks of hair) and diary text. Courtesy of the artist.

seer'.[20] This characterization is in keeping with Charcot's own disposition towards the visual. Charcot is famous for his appointment of a resident photographer to photograph the hysterics who inhabited the famed Salpêtrière clinic.[21] For many of the women, Charcot's linking of hysteria with the photographs caused them to image themselves as one with the clinical pictures. Their identity became so determined by the camera that they performed according to the doctor's expectations. The best 'performers' were rewarded with more photographs taken and became the 'stars' of Salpêtrière.[22] Blanche Wittmann, the famous 'Queen of Hysterics', along with other such successful performers, were featured in Charcot's publications and drew crowds at the *Salpêtrière Bal de Folles*.[23] Many were hypnotized and exhibited at his popular lectures. Augustine, the most famous of Charcot's hysterics, was so frequently photographed that 'elle avait cessè de voir les couleurs; *elle voyait tout en noir et blanc*'.[24]

The reality of the photograph was used not only to index the hysteria of the patient, but also to give the patient a model of how to represent herself. (All the clinicians were male and most of the patients photographed appear to be women.[25]) The women of Salpêtrière were encouraged to see themselves as pure image – as artwork carved out by a Frankensteinian Pygmalion, housed not in an artist's studio, but in an asylum. It is no wonder, then, that in 1862, when Jean-Martin Charcot became the head of the Salpêtrière clinic in Paris, he described it and its five thousand inmates as a 'living museum of pathology'.[26] Charcot's 'museum', as is suggested by both his own account and by Freud's, became a kind of art institute in which the power play between the male artist and his female model/muse was played out on both her body and her mind.

Probing still deeper into the walls of the female body imaged as a waxen Galatea (as a *tabula rasa*, a mystic writing pad), we find that the clinicians of Salpêtrière actually wrote on the bodies of their hysterics with needle-like instruments. They sowed their impressions (in needlepoint), words like '*Démence Précoce*' (Figure 2) or a mysterious date and signature, '*OCT 91 EC*' (Figure 3), or the labelling of '*Satan*' (Figure 4), or the name of the clinic on these anything but patient bodies. These dermagraphed bodies became signed signs of the doctors' own creative visualizations.[27] When the inscriptions became welts and scabs, the doctors read them as proof of the hysteria that they had already diagnosed long ago. As clinical artists, sorcerers of sorts, these doctors claimed that many of the lurid inscriptions appeared unassisted. Or, if they acknowledged assistance, they attributed the 'unnatural' bubbling up to excessive sensitivity to the slightest touch: a hypersensitivity that was simply understood as a blossom of the patient's hysteria. The doctors took the vision to be demonstrative truth. The dermagraphed skin (which inevitably recalls the branding of black slaves in America, the tattooing of Holocaust victims in Germany, and many of the other horrors of body scarring that have marked the other in history) was read as a representation of the patient's hysteria – itself a representation of woman's diseased body. (Phelan writes of another way in which the skin is read symptomatically: 'The focus on skin as the visible marker of race is itself a form of feminizing those races which are not white. Reading the body as the sign of identity is the way men regulate the bodies of women.'[28]) Dermagraphism is a focus on skin that determines those who are not male (hysterics), not sane, not same.

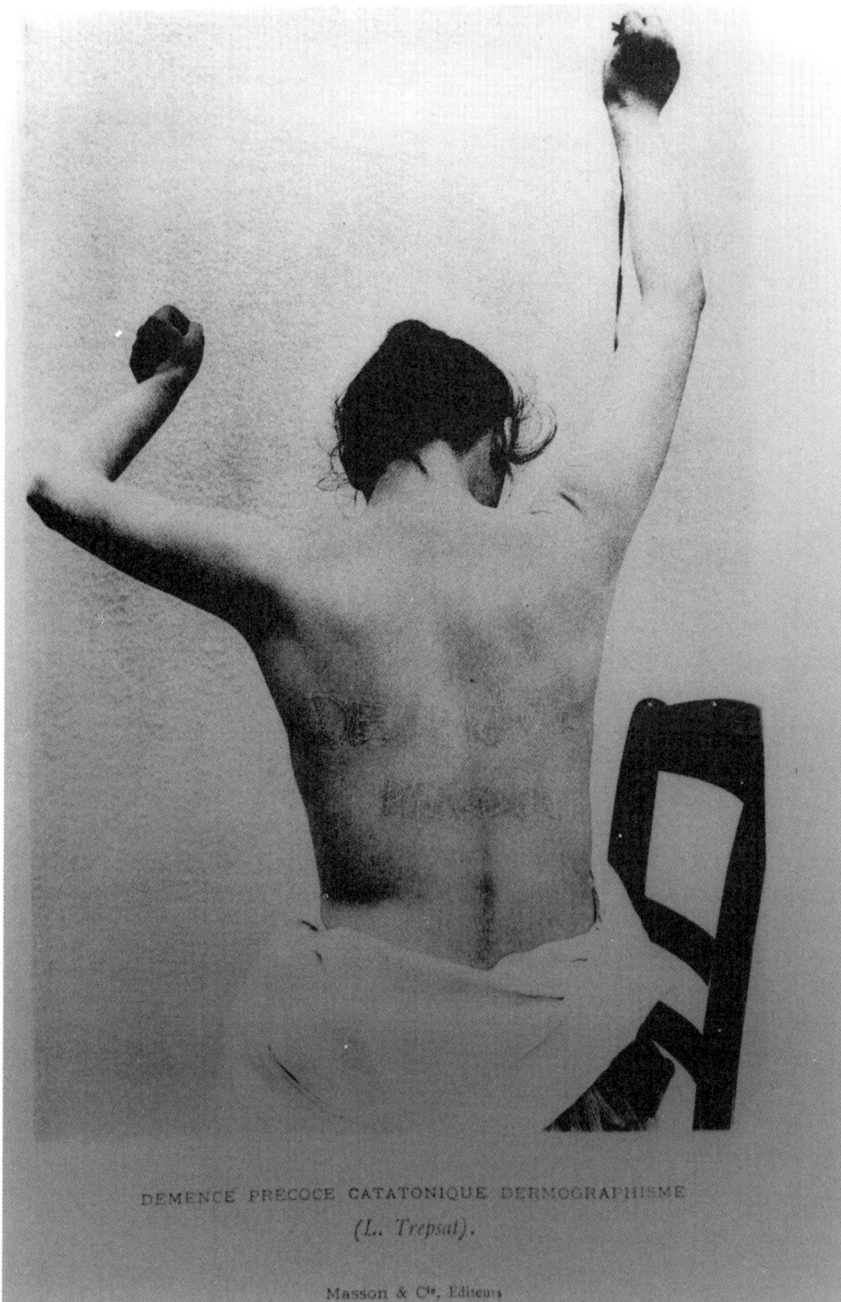

Figure 2 *Démence Précoce*, c. 1904 (*Nouvelle Iconographie de la Salpêtrière*, T. XVII. P1. XXVII)

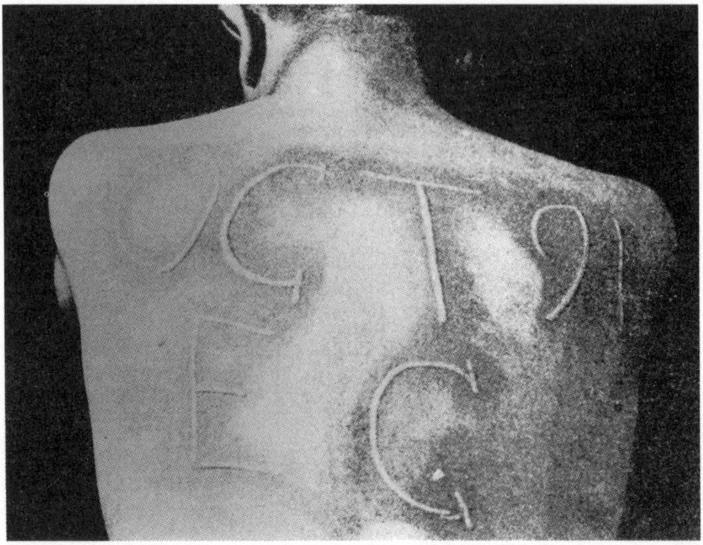

Figure 3 *OCT 91 EC, 1891* (*Journal des maladies cutanées et syphilitiques*, T III)

The dis-eased bodies were then photographed, so that the truth could be seen. Though not a photographer, Charcot himself pledged the truth of his findings by claiming that he was able to see like a camera: '*Mais à la vérité, je ne suis absolument là que le photographe; j'inscris ce que vois.*'[29] Albert Londe, Charcot's director of photography, reiterated the point when he said, '*La plaque photographique est la vraie rétine du savant.*'[30]

The truth content of the pictures from Salpêtrière depended on photography's relationship to the real, its indexical relationships to a referent.[31] Accordingly, like footprints in the sand, the photograph always shares an actual contiguity or connection to the world. Photographs (unlike paintings) require that the picture's referent (the woman and her dermagraphing skin) be there in front of the artist/camera. Roland Barthes has written extensively on the mysterious relationship between a photograph and its referent.[32] In *Camera Lucida*, he finds a tortured, erotic beauty in the photograph's indexicality:

> It is as if the Photograph always carries its referent with itself, both affected by the same amorous or funeral immobility, at the very heart of the moving world: they are glued together, limb by limb, like the condemned man and the corpse in certain tortures; or even like those pairs of fish (sharks, I think according to Michelet) which navigate in convoy, as though united in eternal coitus.[33]

This is the magic of photography, what Barthes describes elsewhere as an ability to develop a 'message without a code'. Yet the paradox of the photograph

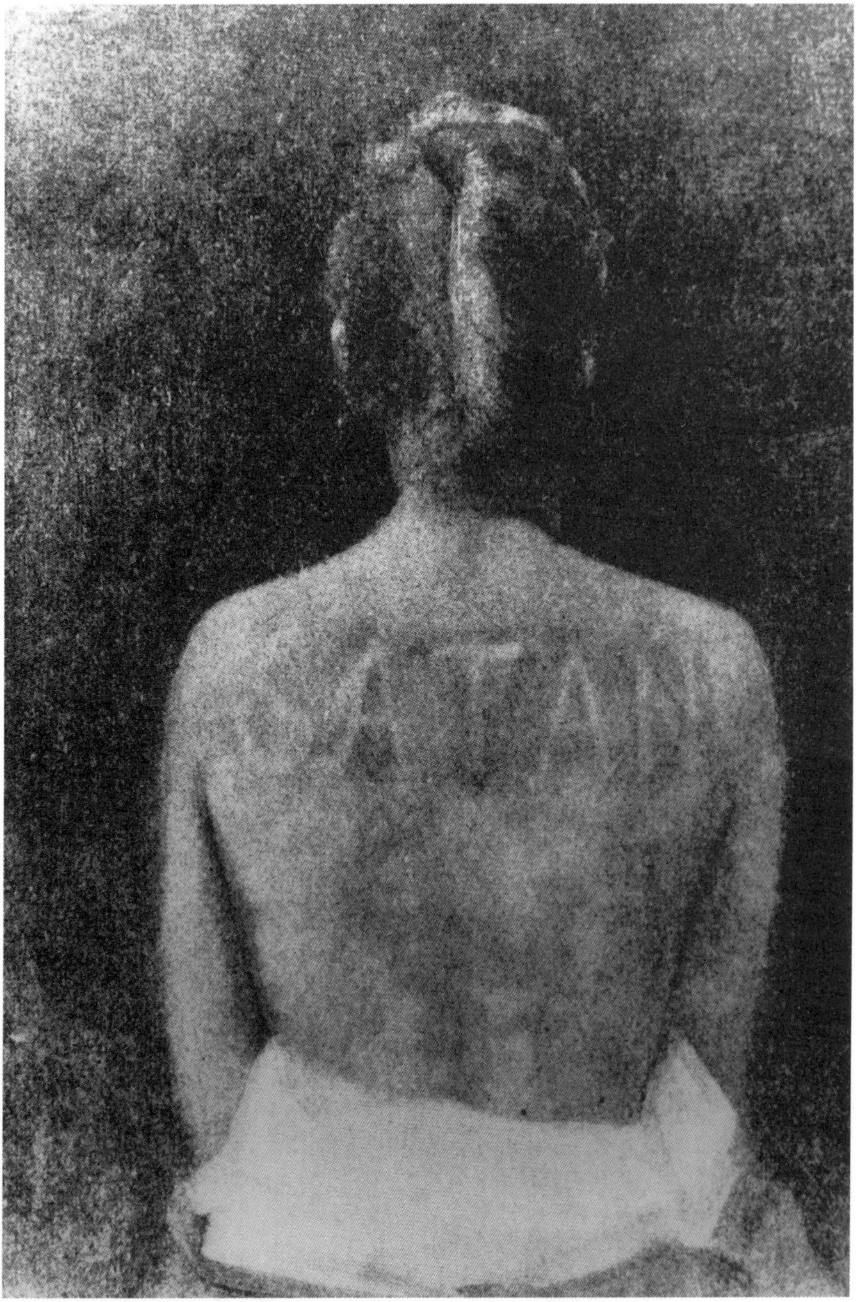

Figure 4 *Satan*, c. 1904 (*Nouvelle Iconographie de la Salpêtrière*)

is that it also develops this 'message without a code' alongside a 'message with a code': it magically pursues its referent while dwelling on the material codes of shading, focus, scale, etc.[34] Like the portmanteau (a large leather travelling bag that opens up into two compartments – or even like portmanteau double-words), the photograph encases (and blends) two different codes: the magical, denoted message without a code and the artful, connoted message with a code.

I have always been struck by the artistic treatment of the dermagraphic photographs. For instance, the surreal beauty in the picture-body that rose to completion on '*OCT 91*' complemented by the doctor's monogram 'EC' (Figure 3).[35] Each carefully inscribed letter, evenly spaced across her back as if her body were a fine piece of thick white cotton paper, as if the doctor were making art. The serifs on each letter 'C' are incomprehensibly cruel – extra strokes of unfathomable callousness – tiny marks of horrific, carefully carried out artistry. Relentlessly tied to the conventions of fine art, the photograph's dramatic casting of lights and darks artistically emphasizes the curve of the patient's strong shoulders, the curvaceous form of an ornamental ear (a starlit moon with its own dark shadow), and the grand sweep of an embossed back. Cropped to perfection, the photograph invites the desire to caress. Like '*Démence précoce*' (Figure 2) or '*Satan*' (Figure 4), it has the kind of beauty prescribed by nineteenth-century French art: a bather painted by Jean Auguste Dominique Ingres or a nude photographed by Eugène Durieu and posed by Eugène Delacroix (Figure 5).

In '*Démence Précoce*', the woman looks as if she could be performing some strange exercise for Eadweard Muybridge; she too is positioned before a camera that seeks to capture both science and art. Like the '*OCT 91*' figure, like a woman pictured by Muybridge, this woman looks (paradoxically) strong and healthy. Catatonic, she is held by the flash and by the disease. Which came first?[36] Again, I am captivated by the artistry of the picture's space. A left elbow forms a toppled over 'V' (sprinkled with bright light) that veeringly points outward beyond the picture's edge. Similarly, a slightly bent right elbow subtly pushes at the opposite edge. At the top of the page the woman's tightly clutched right hand (a fistful of dark grey shadows) holds a long black ribbon (?). Our eye travels downward along the path of the twisted satin line towards the bare breasts that we cannot see: the site of the woman's obscured gaze. Centred, I become lost in the uncaught tendrils of her hair. Those strands of hair touch my own neck and face. (As I type these letters, I catch sight of my own loose strands.) The woman's hair becomes my Barthian 'punctum': a detail which wounds me, which pricks me, which pierces me with personal significance – a detail that I can feel. As he describes his experience of viewing the great range of photographs that draw his attention in *Camera Lucida*, Barthes is similarly pricked by the 'punctum' of 'one child's bad teeth', a 'little boy's huge Danton collar, the girl's finger bandage', the 'necklace (a slender ribbon of braided gold)', a 'kilted groom', an artist's hands with 'slightly repellent . . . spatulate nails, at once soft and hard-edged'.[37] In the

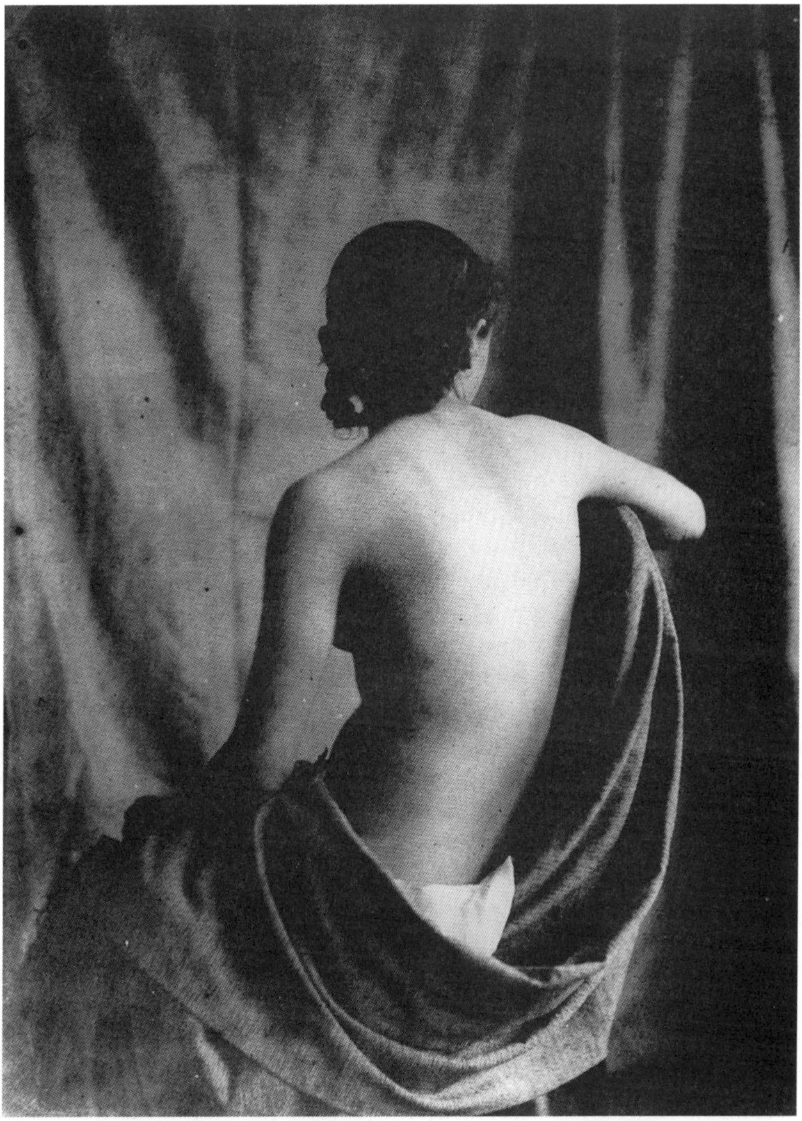

Figure 5 Eugène Durieu and Eugène Delacroix *Draped Model*, c. 1854.

same way that these photographs seems to have chosen Barthes, '*Démence Précoce*' has chosen me.

Yet, despite the beauty of these pictures, the dermagraphed inscriptions wound me so deeply that they *should* outstrip the pleasures of punctum. Still, I take pleasure in looking at them. I am sickened by my own pleasure. Unlike Barthes, I cannot simply claim to 'dismiss all knowledge, all culture . . . to refuse to inherit anything from another eye than my own.'[38] The photographs wound me with horrific visions. My body cringes at the pain of each letter/number written. I long to understand the images as only paper, the bodies as only waxen tablets: my mind's eye attempts to lift the top sheet of the *Wunderblock* in order to wipe the slate, their bodies, clean. But to no avail. The images, even when not before my eyes, remain etched in my mind. The images hurt. Their bodies scrape at mine. The photo-graphs me.[39] The light of the picture writes me: we (the women-referents and me) share light like skin. Balzac feared losing thin ghosts of himself, like layers of skin, with each photograph 'taken'.[40] Maybe it was Balzac who inspired Barthes to write:

> The photograph is literally an emanation of the referent. From a real body, which was there, proceeds radiations which ultimately touch me, who am here; the duration of the transmission is insignificant; the photograph of the missing being, as Sontag says, will touch me like the delayed rays of a star. A sort of umbilical cord links the body of the photographed thing to my gaze: light, though impalpable, is here a carnal medium, a skin I share with anyone who has been photographed.

But this skin has been rubbed with salt. It makes my eyes smart. Luce Irigaray writes, 'In a certain way nothing is as sensitive to touch as my sight.'[41]

Akin to Man Ray's woman as a violin (*Le Violin d'Ingres*, 1924: Figure 6), these picture-body hieroglyphics prefigure all the convulsive beauty and all the violence of surrealism. It is no wonder that the surrealist journal, *La Révolution Surréaliste* (no. 11, 1928), celebrated the fiftieth anniversary of hysteria by reprinting 'six large photographs drawn from the *Iconographie de la Salpêtrière*, showing Charcot's star patient, Augustine, in various "attitudes passionelles".'[42]

While all systems of representation may be composed of signs, the visual has been used most effectively to signify women's difference as her inferiority. Visual signs have authority: they do not easily disappear; they endure time; they take time to fade away. Moreover, they share the representational status of someone who speaks 'the truth' for another who is apparently incapable of self-representation – like the lawyer who represents the accused, or the guardian who represents the child. Or like the dermagraphed women of Salpêtrière who were *sentenced* by their doctors: faceless, they *appear* incapable of speaking. Men look (and act); women appear (as objects).[43] In these photographs, the women are represented not as individuals (these pictures are not portraits), but as objects without sensate bodies. The materiality of their actual bodies has been replaced by the media of photography. They are all paper and chemicals.[44]

The power of the doctor's gaze, masculinist, objectifying and monological, is preternaturally real in the Salpêtrière photographs. The pictures are a horrific exaggeration of the nudes painted, sculpted and photographed throughout the history of art. As Johannes Fabian has so powerfully argued in *Time and the Other*, visualism, in its most abstract and general form, is a monological discourse that

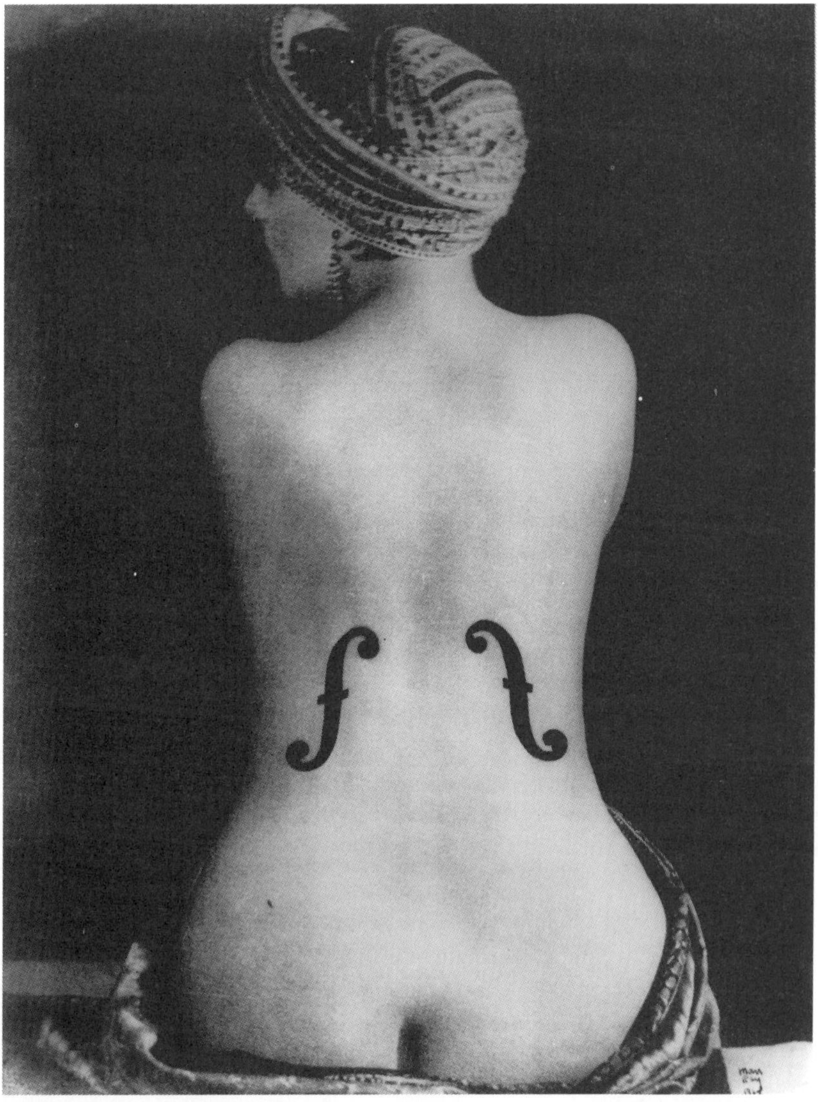

Figure 6 Man Ray; *Le Violin d'Ingres,* 1924 (c) 1998 Man Ray Trust/Artist's Rights Society, NY/ADAGP, Paris

denies a language of difference, and thereby paints over the possibility of the heterological, constructing difference as sameness and as lacking. That is why we are encouraged to understand, to 'see' the other through a theory of knowledge which turns on 'visualism', so much so 'that the ability to "visualize" a culture or society almost becomes synonymous for understanding it'.[45]

Freudian psychoanalytic thought stands at the centre of modern Western testimonies on concepts of sexual difference, and is rooted in this 'one-eyed' concept of visualism. Such 'homological' visions are part and parcel of the always absent but continually inscribed feminine. Like the patient at Salpêtrière who is identified only as 'W', whose stomach gave rise to the letters of the clinic.[46] Like Rebecca in Hitchcock's famous film, who is only seen in the form of a cursive 'R' that relentlessly appears on her fetishized things – from her monogrammed satin pillows and lingerie to the top of her stationery. 'R' is everywhere, but *she* is nowhere to be seen. 'R' for Rebecca; 'R' for Freud's Miss Lucy R; 'R' for Representation; 'R' for the Rhetoric of visualism.

Undoing the primacy of visualism: or, smelling with Freud

Despite Freud's usual emphatic privileging of a masculine, homological, monological standard of sight, it appears that difference permeates his *Civilization and its Discontents* in a most unexpected and non-visual way. This text is, in fact, riddled with *sexual difference discontent*, which is articulated through olfactory marginalia. In two footnotes, whose excessive length signals trouble, sexual difference bleeds into the body of the text as 'the difference between the senses of smell and sight'.[47]

In the first fetid footnote, we learn that civilized culture's 'diminution of the olfactory stimuli' was (as Jane Gallop has termed it) 'a triumph of the eye over the nose'.[48] In the past, lowly man was sexually stimulated by the smells of menstruation – but no longer . . . thanks to his evolved preference for looking, not smelling. In Freud's words:

> Visual excitations, which in contrast to the intermittent olfactory stimuli, were able to maintain a permanent effect. . . . The diminution of the olfactory stimuli seems itself to be a consequence of man's raising himself from the ground, of his assumption of an upright gait; this made his genitals, which were previously concealed, visible.[49]

Later in the same footnote, Freud calls up all our vulgar associations of women with dogs by stipulating:

> It would be incomprehensible . . . that man should use the name of his most faithful friend in the animal world – the dog – as a term of abuse if that creature had not incurred his contempt through two characteristics: that it is an animal whose dominant sense is that of smell and one which has no horror of excrement, and that it is not ashamed of its sexual functions.[50]

Erect man gazes ahead and walks all over the smell of woman. But is it such a triumph? Gallop jokes: 'The penis may be more visible, but female genitalia have a stronger smell.'[51]

Freud summed up his perspective on women and smell best while within the second fetid footnote of *Civilization and its Discontents*, where he claimed 'that neurotics, and many others besides, take exception to the fact that "*inter urinas et faeces nascimur*" [we are born between urine and faeces]'.[52] In other words, for Freud, the child smells the mother seeing her: smell comes before seeing. Neurotics and hysterics have simply failed at repressing the mother and her smell. After all, as Freud argued, a 'memory stinks just as an actual object may stink' unless it is effectively repressed.[53] As a result, Freud claimed the childlike tendency to take pleasure in smell plays a significant part in the genesis of neurosis.[54] This is why the feet and the hair, particularly odorous body parts, make such perfect fetish objects for the neurotic; they recall the body of the mother and the coprophilic pleasures of a long lost childhood. Of course, as Freud tells us, not any foot can be a treasured fetish, for it is 'only dirty and evil-smelling feet [that] become sexual objects'.[55]

While not all of Freud's patients with overdetermined relationships with smell were women, many of them were, and Freud likened a 'heightened sense of smell' with hysteria, a disease that predominantly affected women. Dora was supposedly disgusted by Herr K's kiss, not so much because his 'member' became erect, but because it could be associated with the smell and 'the function of micturition'.[56] Miss Lucy R had entirely lost her ability to smell, yet was continually haunted and pursued by one olfactory sensation after another. First, there was the smell of burnt pudding, and then (after Freud cured her of that) the smell of cigar smoke.[57] But the bottom line for Freud was that no matter who smelled what, it had something to do with the mother/feminine. Smell was to the feminine what the visual was to the masculine: odour, indeed, separated the girls from the boys.

Of course, all this nosy stuff appears particularly Freudian, given Freud's own relationship to Dr Fliess, the ear, nose and throat man who could attribute almost any disorder to the nose. In one letter to Fliess, Freud went so far as to suggest that the 'development' of man's upright carriage was connected with the common phrase, 'He turns up his nose' – meaning of course that a man with an erect nose regards himself as something particularly noble.[58] The relationship between these two 'noble men' is surely the subject of another text. However, we can safely say that Freud's essay and letters suggest that though we may not see her, we can certainly smell her.

The relationship between 'woman' and smell, so deeply rooted in Freud, is constructed as an atavistic throwback to signify not only the feminine, but also the primitive. Such a Darwinian spin on smell was also emphasized by one of Freud's contemporaries: Havelock Ellis, the great 'sexologist'. Ellis devoted an entire chapter to smell in his *Studies in the Psychology of Sex, Volume IV* (1905).[59]

As might be expected, Ellis located an excess of 'smell' in the dark races: 'Odor,' he said, '[seems] to be correlated to some extent with intensity of pigmentation, as well as hairiness.'[60] As a result, Ellis repeatedly described the smell of peoples that he regraded as lower on the evolutionary scale as musky. For him, musk was an animalistic and deeply sexual smell. 'Musk,' said Ellis, 'is the odor which not only in the animals to which it has given a name [musk-rat, musk-ox, etc.], but in many others, is a specifically sexual odor, chiefly emitted during the sexual season. The sexual odors indeed, of most animals seem to be modifications of musk.'[61] Ellis specifically relates the smell of animalistic musk to black women, to lactating women, to women in general, to the Chinese, and even to the demented.[62]

Following the kind of thinking that characterizes Ellis's study, musk had lost its hold as a 'perfume'. By the time of Ellis's post-Darwinian study, white European culture was fully invested in ridding itself of any associations, smell or otherwise, with a 'primitive' animal past. Musk-like smells that had once been used with enthusiasm were now forsaken for flowery perfumes – and smell as a modern civility was invented. According to Alain Corbin in *The Foul and the Fragrant*,

> Western man and woman would henceforth endeavor with increasing skill to disguise body odors that had become burdensome; it was a way of denying the sexual role of the sense of smell, or at least shifting the field of olfactory stimulation and allusion; thereafter it fell to the delicate exhalations of perspiration, and not to the powerful odors of secretions, to presage the intimate liaison.[63]

A performance guided by the *odor di femina*

In the history of sight and smell, photography – like flowery perfumes – disguises visual odours, the sweet stench of which seeps out of Freud's margins (pushed there by a text that otherwise constitutes a monument against smell) and into Lacan's theory of the gaze as *objet petit a*. For Lacan, the gaze as *objet petit a* operates alongside (not above) such other activities of the body as smelling, writing, touching and expelling babies and faeces. And insofar as this is true, Lacan offers us a gaze configured in movement rather than fixation. The gaze's nose is no longer turned up.[64]

The gaze as *objet petit a* describes a relation of loss between the body and its 'objects' articulated in the dynamics of desire: the baby drops out of the mother's body; song comes from deep within our diaphragm and coos out of tightened lips; a tear eases itself out of a duct and seeps out through a tiny pinkened pinpricked hole, a gaze falls out of the eye. All these little things emphasize erotogenic rims of our own bodies (mouth, anus, nose, eyes, ears, genitals), off which falls some bit of one's own otherness – a little other, an *autre*, like the one falling off Lacan's own phrase '*objet petit a[utre]*', and fills up some of the lack in an other, who then expels yet another little object, creating yet another hole to be filled, and so on. As a result, we desire to have our holes filled up and we desire to fill up the holes of others. Yet every time we release an *objet* or two, we create more holes in our own bodies and then desire more *objets* from others. Lacan's story of the *objet petit a* is a never-ending story: desire only creates more desire.[65]

Lacan says in *Television*:

> A gaze, that of Beatrice – that is to say, three times nothing, a fluttering of the eyelids and the exquisite trash that results from it – and there emerges that Other whom we only identify through her *jouissance*: her whom he, Dante, cannot satisfy, because from her, he can have only this look, only this object, but of whom he tells us that God fulfills her utterly; it is precisely by receiving the assurance of that from her own mouth that he arouses us.[66]

Beatrice's gaze flies out of her eyes, with a fluttering of her erotogenic eyelids. The gaze is tossed away (like trash) and it drives Dante mad. He tries to fill himself up with Beatrice's trash. (Desire may feed on waste, but it cannot fill itself up with it.) He cannot get enough. He can only get this look. Dante tells us that God fulfils Beatrice utterly: sounds/words are being released from his lips: the erotogenic rims of his mouth. We, in turn, become aroused: we take in the trash and let more out.

For Lacan, the emphasis is on the little thing itself (the gaze, the word) *and* on the movement of the taking in of the *objet* as it becomes absorbed into the subject. The *objet petit a* is special: it initiates and takes pleasure in movement. Quite simply, one might say that the space of the *object petit a* is not static, but rather *performative*. This emphasis on movement serves to separate Lacan's *objet petit a* from Freud's fetish.

Inevitably, the boundaries between the fetish and the *objet petit a* are blurred.[67] They are almost synonyms. Their undecidable relationship is typically Lacanian and elusive (like a haunting aroma). Yet, even if one senses that the separation of Freud's fetish from Lacan's *objet petit a* is merely an academic exercise in splitting hairs, one cannot overlook the fact that fetishism is associated with neurosis, while the game of the *objet petit a* is not; it is desire itself.

Like Lacan, I am interested in the *odor di femina* as a frutiful *objet petit a*. Lacan's mysterious *odor di femina* exudes most memorably from his 'Seminar on "The Purloined Letter"'. According to Lacan, when in 'The Purloined Letter, the Minister steals the letter from the Queen, he also takes possession of the sign of woman (Queen), and thereby becomes possessed by woman's sign, becomes castrated, becomes Queen.' 'He is obliged to don the role of the Queen, and even the attributes of femininity', and so to un-become a man or to become an 'unbecoming man.'[68] According to Lacan, one can smell 'the oddest *odor di femina*' whenever the (queer or) unbecoming Minister appears.[69] This odour seems to exude from the text, causing the reader's eyes to water; the tears (the *objets*) that fall/follow obscure the page. Lacan compares the search for the invisible letter (that lies right before everyone's eyes) to the experience of trying to read 'large letters spaced out widely across a map'; your eyes simply cannot *see* the country's name.[70] In Lacan's wild interpretation of Poe's tale, the stolen letter is read 'like an immense female body' that no one can see (but you can smell her).[71]

Lacan's use of the phrase *odor di femina* recalls Don Giovanni's own nose trap when he first smells *it* during the first act of Mozart's opera.This unseen odour of 'woman' sets Giovanni off on an endless series of foreplayic seductions, as he travels on an odoriferous trail towards the mysterious *odor di femina*: a feminine *bouquet garni* lost somewhere in the soup pot. But smell plays a cruel trick on Giovanni. Following *her* scent leaves *him* chasing his own tail in an endless circle. Once the cheesecloth is torn apart, it turns out that the aroma is nothing but a common, well-known herb: the familiar smell of his own wife – the woman that he wanted to avoid at all costs.

Likewise, Catherine Clément suggests that Lacan, too, was guided by the *odor di femina* when he was searching for the meaning of Diego Velázquez's *Las Meninas* (Figure 7). We might thus conclude that Lacan, like Don Giovanni, was guided by something unseen. According to Clément:

> Lacan had first greeted Foucault's admirable chapter on the subject with enthusiasm [as appears in *The Order of Things*]. But he quickly changed the subject and eventually produced his own commentary on *Las Meninas*, guided as always by the 'odor di femina.' The object that occupies the geometric center of the canvas is not the king or the queen [as Foucault had argued] but rather, hidden beneath an enormous hoopskirt, the infanta's genitalia.[72]

Clément tells us that Lacan knew that even if it were possible to lift up the pounds of petticoats and the heavy armature of the infanta's hoopskirt, her secret parts, her letter(s), would always remain obscured.[73] For the *odor di femina* that she emanates is doubly unseen. This conception of the doubly unseen is not unlike the double-sided painting (un)pictured in *Las Meninas*: we can see the back of the painting's stretched canvas and we can see the painting's painted subject (a double portrait of the king and queen) reflected in the mirror hanging on the back wall – but we cannot see the *actual* painting: it is doubly unseen. Compounding the visual confusion that takes place when a representation is nothing more than a representation of representation, *Las Meninas* describes a multitude of traditional pictorial frames that have been used throughout the history of painting. Within the rectangular pictorial surface (in addition to the back of the canvas,

Figure 7 Diego Velázquez; *Las Meninas*, 1656 Museo del Prado, Madrid

criss-crossed and framed by stretcher bars, and in addition to the looking-glass, which reflects the painting of the king and queen on the canvas's other side that we cannot see), the walls are covered with many other paintings (including two by Rubens) and the back wall features an open doorway flooded with light that frames a member of the queen's staff, but could be an image of *Velázquez* in masquerade. As Foucault has argued, *Las Meninas* is subjectless: it is pure representation. The painting reveals nothing. Yet, for Lacan there is a subject: our own annihilated subjectivity.

Lacan tells us that a painting annihilates us by looking back at us, without including us in the 'picture'. As Lacan has remarked, 'The picture is in my eye.

But I am not in the picture.'[74] This is, of course, in reference to Lacan's famous recollection of being out at sea with some fishermen. While staring at a bit of flotsam (more trash) that had floated by – a sardine can – one of the fishermen exclaims (to Lacan): '*You see that can? Do you see it? Well it doesn't see you!*'[75] The fisherman's statement, riddled with irony, is poking fun at Lacan. The fisherman is illustrating how Lacan is 'rather out of place in the picture',[76] out on a fishing boat in the middle of the sea. For among 'those fellows who were earning their livings with great difficulty,' Lacan 'looked like *nothing* on earth'[77] – not unlike the flotsam floating on the surface of the waves. The 'joke' disturbed Lacan. For, seeing himself as the fishermen saw him, as a bit of garbage, as nothing, annihilated his perspective and so his self/subjectivity.

In Lacan's scheme of things, looking annihilates us by emphasizing our own inability to see. For, even when looking at a painting, we too are looked at from all sides, yet we are unaware of who is looking at us and from what point. And it is in this way that even an inanimate object, like the sardine can, or the infanta, or even the infanta's dress, actually does look back at us, but in such a way as to empower the object itself and not the viewer. It annihilates us. As a result, our gaze within its constructed socialization (as primary, as the only *true* sense) always falls short – like the perspective lines travelling towards the geometric centre of *Las Meninas*. In Lacan's words, 'I see only from one point, but in my existence I am looked at from all sides.'[78] Norman Bryson expands upon this point by adding 'that the subject who sees is no more the center of visual experience than the subject of language'.[79] Our eyes/'I's are empty receptacles, like mirrors, that provide the material for misrecognition, to fulfil our mythic fantasies of being able to see, to speak. The infanta's dress becomes the clothing of a horrific idea: our own annihilation. As a result, her dress veils death's head and operates not unlike the oblique form that troubles, pulsates, dazzles and spreads out between Hans Holbein's *Ambassadors* (Figure 8): an anamorphic form that traps the gaze and trapped Lacan. (Lacan has written more about this painting than any other; it was his 'woman-scent' answer to Foucault's treatment of *Las Meninas*.)[80]

After walking around the room, after tilting your head in just the right way, you may apprehend Holbein's form – but what is it? A skull – empty eye sockets – glorious nothingness. In the words of Lacan, 'All this shows at the very heart of the period in which the subject emerged and geometrical optics was an object of research, Holbein makes visible for us here something that is simply the subject as annihilated' or 'our own nothingness in the figure of the death's head'.[81] Similarly, by approaching the canvas of *Las Meninas*, by nearly touching my nose to the canvas, a photographic detail of the cluster of roses that graces the infanta's lovely dress causes me to exclaim: 'Why there is nothing there at all!' (Figure 9).

But in approaching her dress as if vision were primary, I am forgetting that, for Lacan, there is a split between vision and the gaze. Vision is just one small part of the gaze as *objet petit a* and therefore must be considered in relationship to other *objets* that fall from our noses, lips and ears. For Lacan, the gaze is

Figure 8 18-41 Hans Holbein the Younger, *The French Ambassadors*, 1533. Reproduced by courtesy of the Trustees of the National Gallery, London

a polyvalent category, like thought itself. Lacan's gaze is not only a seen gaze. Recall Lacan detects that 'A wild odour emanates . . .' from the 'function of *seeingness*'.[82] Lacan's gaze is a sensate gaze that we can also smell or hear. Lacan finds an example of the latter in Sartre's *Being and Nothingness*:

> If you turn to Sartre's own text, you will see that, far from speaking of the emergence of this gaze as of something that concerns the organ of sight, he refers to the *sound* of the rustling of leaves, suddenly heard while out hunting, to a footstep heard in a corridor. And when are these sounds heard? At the moment when he has presented himself in the action of looking through a keyhole.[83]

Figure 9 Diego Velázquez, *Las Meninas* (detail), 1656

Sartre's text, as presented by Lacan, leaves me blind with a key. I am blinded by sounds that are part of a polyvalent gaze that becomes my tiny key(hole): my *objet petit a*.

More than a gaze

Page duBois writes: 'If theory is a gaze, feminist theory must be more than a gaze at the same object, more than finding a new sameness.'[84] For me, duBois' words are doused with a slight fragrance, an odour of difference, that fosters my decision to make such a big stink about Lacan's passing reference to the *odor di femina*. I am not the only one who has lingered over Lacan's enigmatic use of this odd Italian phrase. Clément returns to it several times in *The Lives and Legends of Jacques Lacan* and Michèle Montrelay (possibly echoing Lacan) claims that femininity speaks *odor di femina*: an immediate, unmediated mode that no one can forget, a stinky language (not of flowers) that calls back to our first connections with the body of the mother.[85] Yet, perhaps Lacan's text is smellier from his one-time mention of the *odor di femina* than one might think. It doesn't take much. The *odor di femina* may be fragile, but its essence, 'tiny and almost impalpable', is enduring.[86]

Lacan's one drop of *odor di femina* loosens the gaze into an expanded constellation of senses. No longer overcome by the look, bodies come into play . . . 'a wild odour emanates'. I, like Lacan (and apart from Freud), am interested in 'a triumph of the gaze over the eye'.[87] Turning back the pages of my text with my fingers, my eyes and my nose, the pictures elicit their own odd *odor di femina*. I smell detergent, sweat, vomit, the mother's tears, the child's sobs in the swatch of Mary Kelly's son's baby blanket. In the dermagraphic pictures from Salpêtrière, I am overcome by the smells of stale blood, sickness, fear, attacked skin, sour skin, sterilized sheets, not so recently washed hair, the armpit of a raised arm, the nervous breath of a frightened woman, skin, skin, skin. Durieu's and Delacroix's draped model smells of flowery perfume. Their photograph (which plays sensual havoc with the curve of her back, the glimpse of her left breast, and the thin, tight braid that wraps loosely around her head and falls, just right, at the nape of her neck) is painted with 'the texture of perfume'.[88] In contrast, the picture's black dots (photographic accidents), which speckle the fabric backdrop and the drapery that wraps the chair and the model's lovely body as one, are signs of acrid loss. The black spots mar the vision. They mar the sweet perfume. *Le Violin d'Ingres* smells of the resin that I used to gently rub on the hair of the bow to the violin that I would never play. Its visual smell is screechingly odd, disturbing and humorous. *Las Meninas* smells of the secrets of little girls and the overwhelming scent of a big dog. Close up, *Las Meninas* smells of cadmium white, vermilion, ivory black, the hairs of a paintbrush, canvas, turpentine and linseed oil: exciting and noxious. The French ambassadors smell of knowledge, privilege, taste . . . like a library or a museum or a man's beard: their smell attempts, but only attempts, to mask the *odor di femina* that emanates from the eye sockets of the skull that spins along the canvas's bottom edge.

By releasing Hope's 'wild odour', my purloined images have stolen me. Though you may not see her (Hope) in Kelly's *Post-partum Document*, in the dermagraphed women from Salpêtrière, in Man Ray's *Le Violin d'Ingres*, in Durieu's and Delacroix's *Draped Model*, in Velázquez's *Las Meninas*, or in Holbein's *The French Ambassadors* . . . you can certainly smell her.

Notes

1 Muriel Rukeyser, 'Myth', in *The Collected Poems* (New York: McGraw-Hill, 1978), p. 498, emphasis added. Teresa de Lauretis uses Rukeyser's wonderful recasting of the Oedipus myth to conclude her own enlightening chapter on the complex relationship between Oedipus, narrative, gender, sadism, desire, cinema. See 'Desire in Narrative', in *Alice Doesn't: Feminism, Semiotics, Cinema* (Bloomington: Indiana University Press, 1984), p. 157.

2 Jacques Lacan, *The Four Fundamental Concepts of Psycho-analysis*, ed. Jacques-Alain Miller, trans. Alan Sheridan (New York: Norton, 1978), p. 82. First published in French as *Le séminaire de Jacques Lacan*, Livre XI, 'Les quatre concepts fondamentaux de la psychanalyse' (Paris: Éditions du Seuil, 1973).

3 Peggy Phelan, *Unmarked: the Politics of Performance* (London and New York: Routledge, 1993), p. 5.

4 Ibid., p. 1.

5 The final chapter of Phelan's *Unmarked* is entitled 'Afterword: notes on hope'. Phelan, who also takes on the fecundity of Hope, writes, 'We perform Hope but we do not perhaps believe enough in her any longer. What would it take to *be* her rather than (merely?) enact her, resist her, flirt with her?' (p. 178). The phrase 'the rustle of language' belongs to Barthes. Barthes unravels it in glorious, bountiful, beautiful, rustling yardage as follows:

> The rustle of language forms a utopia. Which utopia? That of a music of meaning; in its utopic state, language would be enlarged, I should even say *denatured* to the point of forming a vast auditory fabric in which the semantic apparatus would be made unreal; the phonic, metric, vocal signifier would be deployed in all its sumptuosity, without a sign ever becoming detached from it (ever *naturalizing* this pure layer of delectation), but also – and this is what is difficult – without meaning being brutally dismissed, dogmatically foreclosed, in short castrated . . . when attributed to the machine, the rustle is only the noise of an absence of noise, in the same way, shifted to language, it would be that meaning which reveals an exemption of meaning or – the same thing – that non-meaning which produces in the distance a meaning henceforth liberated from all the aggressions of which the sign, formed in the 'sad and fierce history of men,' is the Pandora's box.
>
> ('The rustle of language', in *The Rustle of Language*, trans. Richard Howard (Berkeley and Los Angeles: University of California Press, 1989), pp. 77–8. Originally published in French as *Le bruissement de la langue* (Paris: Editions du Seuil, 1983))

6 David Knowles, *The Secrets of the Camera Obscura* (San Francisco: Chronicle Books, 1994), p. 12; emphasis added.

7 Sigmund Freud, 'Screen memories' (1899) in *The Standard Edition of the Complete Psychological Works of Sigmund Freud*, 24 vols, ed. and trans. James Strachey (London: Hogarth Press, 1953–74), vol. 3: 301–22.

8 Sigmund Freud, *Moses and Monotheism* (1939), in *The Standard Edition*, vol. 23: 1–137.

9 Sigmund Freud, 'A note upon the "mystic writing pad"' (1924), in *The Standard Edition*, vol. 19: 227–34.

10 Rosalind Krauss, *The Optical Unconscious* (Boston, MA: Institute of Technology, 1993), p. 57.

11 Roland Barthes, *Roland Barthes by Roland Barthes* (New York: Farrar, Straus & Giroux, 1922), p. 161. Originally published in French as *Roland Barthes par Roland Barthes* (Paris: Éditions du Seuil, 1975).

12 Martin Jay somewhat disagrees with me, in that he (along with Derrida) sees Freud's work after *The Interpretation of Dreams* (as represented by 'A note upon the "mystic writing pad"') as a 'movement from optical metaphors of the

psyche . . . to more scriptural ones' (*Downcast Eyes: The Denigration of Vision in Twentieth-Century French Thought* (Berkeley and Los Angeles: University of California Press, 1993), p. 335). Unlike Jay, I am simply emphasizing the visuality of script. Of related interest is Krauss' emphasis on the pictorial possibilities of Freud's *Wunderblock*, as it connects to surrealism and an anti-modernist conception of vision. See especially her fabulous discussion of Ernst's *The Master's Bedroom*, 1920 (*The Optical Unconscious*, pp. 54–8).

13 Emily Apter, *Feminizing the Fetish: Psychoanalysis and Narrative Obsession in Turn-of-the-Century France* (Cornell: Cornell University Press, 1991), p. xiii.

14 Ibid., p. 102.

15 Ibid., pp. 100 and 105.

16 Ibid., p. 106.

17 Ibid., p. 106.

18 Leslie Camhi, 'Stealing femininity: department store kleptomania as sexual disorder', *Differences: A Journal of Feminist Cultural Studies*, 5(1) (1993): 39.

19 Apter, *Feminizing the Fetish*, p. 115.

20 Freud observed Charcot and Salpêtrière for one year (1885–6). These words are from an obituary that Freud wrote for Charcot. See Freud, 'Charcot' (1893), *The Standard Edition*, vol. 1, p. 12.

21 Robert Londe was the director of photographic services at Salpêtrière during the 1880s. See Georges Didi-Huberman, *Invention de l'hystérie: Charcot et l'iconographie photographique de la Salpêtrière* (Paris: Macula, 1982), p. 35. The photographs were published along with textual diagnoses in books and serial publications of the period. In his scholarship, Charcot went so far as to relate his own iconograpy of the mentally ill with works from the history of art: 'paintings, mosaics, tapestries, sculptures, icons, and bas-reliefs – which depicted anything to do with epileptics, ecstatics, choreics, possessed, and demoniacs' (A. R. G. Owen, *Hysteria, Hypnosis and Healing: The Work of J. -M. Charcot* (London: Dennis Dobson, 1971), p. 69). Most notable is Charcot's publication, in collaboration with Paul Richer, of *Les démoniaques dans l'art* (1887). The text has been recently republished in a facsimile edition with new commentary: J. M. Charcot and Paul Richer, *Les démoniaques dans l'art, suivi de la foi qui guérit de J. M. Charcot, introduction de Pierre Fédida, postface de Georges Didi-Huberman* (Paris: Macula, 1984).

Photographs had already been used in the field of psychiatry some ten years earlier by Dr Hugh Welch Diamond (Surrey Asylum, England). Diamond, unlike Charcot, actually took pictures of his own (mostly female) hysterical patients. A leading member of the Royal Centre for Photography, he was clearly influenced by the aesthetic tastes of the period. Indeed, Elaine Showalter has written: 'Some of the younger women, with their heavy hair and distracted gaze, resemble the well-known studies of women artistically photographed by Diamond's contemporaries, especially Julia Margaret Cameron or Henry Peach Robinson' (Elaine Showalter, *The Female Malady: Women, Madness and English Culture, 1830–1980* (New York: Pantheon, 1985), p. 87).

22 Didi-Huberman, 'The figurative incarnation of the sentence (notes on the "autographic" skin)', trans. Caryn Davidson, *LAICA Journal* (Los Angeles Institute of Contemporary Art), 5(47) (Spring 1987): 67.

23 Elaine Showalter, *The Female Malady*, p. 148.

24 Didi-Huberman, *Invention de l'hystérie*, p. 108.

25 However, it is important to understand that Charcot felt there was 'no sexual aetiology of hysteria' (Stephen Heath, *The Sexual Fix* (London: Macmillan, 1982), p. 37) and that men were prone to hysteria as well. As Heath puts it, 'There is no sexual aetiology if sexual is to mean some cause in the reproductive organs. [The Greek word *hystera* meaning 'uterus' or 'womb'] But then there are traces, signs, marks of sexual preoccupation, something is at stake in hysteria – in its manifestation, its conception, its representation. Charcot opposes a sexual aetiology in the first sense and then reinscribes the sexual, those traces, throughout his work and practice' (*The Sexual Fix*, p. 37).

26 Didi-Huberman, 'The figurative incarnation of the sentence (notes on the "autographic" skin)', p. 67. Charcot's 'museum work' was played out seemingly in all aspects of his life. Take, for example, the following description of Charcot's consulting room, written by an American who had visited Charcot's clinic at Salpêtrière (C. F. Withington, 'Letter to the Editor', *Boston Medical and Surgical Journal*, 129: 207 (24 August 1893)):

> The walls of this room [the consulting room] are, it is to be feared, calculated to divert the attention of the casual visitor from the cases immediately before us. For on these walls, in fact, almost entirely covering them, is a series of reproductions, photographic and in engraving, of those paintings in which the world's great artists have sought to depict the manifestations of hysteria and hystero-epilepsy. Prominent among them, of course, are pictures of the casting out of devils. Here are seen the demoniac youth from Raphael's Transfiguration and similar figures from the works of other Italian masters and from Rubens. Charcot has evidently made a diligent search through the Italian churches for good pictures embracing the subject and has got together an astonishing array. By way of comparison with these great painters' conceptions of such phenomena is placed a photographic copy of the well-known French picture of Charcot himself exhibiting in his clinic a woman with major hysteria.

27 Dermagraphism was *officially* acknowledged in 1879 by G. Dujardin-Beaumetz, who called it *femme autographique*. See 'Note sur des troubles vasomoteurs de la peau observés sur une hystérique (femme autographique)' in *L'Union médicale* 144 (9 December 1879): 917–22. This text is reprinted with Georges Didi-Huberman's 'Une notion du corps-cliché aux XIXème siècle', *Parachute* 35 (June–August 1984): 13–14. Dujardin-Beaumetz was a medical doctor at Saint-Antoine.

28 Phelan, *Unmarked*, p. 10. Phelan goes on to relate a West Indian folk-tale told by Lorene Carey in *Black Ice*, in which a woman drapes her skin over her chair

before she goes out to enjoy the night. When she returns she is always careful to put her skin back on before her husband wakes. But one night he discovers her escapades and is determined to stop her. An old woman in the village advises him to rub his wife's skin with salt. 'A few nights later, the woman leaves again and the husband applies the salt to her skin. When she returns to her skin it will not yield: "Skin, skin, ya na know me?" she screams. . . . Caught between her body and her spirit, her insides keep her out. The husband who believes he has the right to the entrances and exits of her body can coat the inside of her skin with salt but he cannot keep her home. His failure to hold her in their bed prompts him to make her skin unable to house her spirit . . . she remains lost to her own body because of his desire to mark it as his' (Phelan, *Unmarked*, p. 10). This folk-tale holds the reality of Charcot's dermagraphed women, whose skin is marked, not with salt, but with needles. The effect is dramatically the same: their skin is painfully lost to the men who house them.

29 Charcot, quoted in Didi-Huberman, *Invention de l'hystérie*, p. 32.

30 Londe, quoted in ibid., p. 35.

31 For an excellent discussion of the ways in which photography serves the law as a result of its assumed relationship to reality and to the real, see John Tagg, 'A means of surveillance: the photograph as evidence in law', in *The Burden of Representation: Essays on Photographies and Histories* (London: Macmillan Education, 1988) pp. 66–102.

32 See Roland Barthes, 'The photographic message' (pp. 15–31), 'Rhetoric of the image' (pp. 32–51) and 'The third meaning' (pp. 52–68) in *Image-Music-Text*, trans. Stephen Heath (New York: Hill and Wang, 1977).

33 Roland Barthes, *Camera Lucida*, trans. Richard Howard (New York: Farrar, Straus & Giroux, 1981), pp. 5–6.

34 See Roland Barthes' essay 'The photographic message', in *Image/Music/Text*, pp. 15–31.

35 The name of the doctor was Èlie Châtelain. Didi-Huberman writes: 'Et ce qui s'écrira sur le dos du sujet-cliché ne sera ni plus ni moins que le nom du médecin, le sujet supposé-savoir, qui se rêve alors comme l'artiste, le fictor, l'auteur du sujet. Ainsi, le docteur Èlie Châtelain n'hésitait-il pas à signer et à dater le corps iconique de son sujet-cliché, dans le temps même où, pour le verser au grand musèe de la clinique, il le photographiait' ('Une notion du corps-cliché aux XIXème siècle', p. 13).

36 For a fascinating discussion of how Charcot claimed to use the photographic flash to produce catalepsy (as proof of hysterical neurosis), see Ulrich Baer, 'Photography and hysteria: toward a poetics of the flash', *The Yale Journal of Criticism*, 7(1) (Spring 1994): 41–77.

37 Barthes, *Camera Lucida*, pp. 45, 51, 53 and 57.

38 Ibid., p. 51.

39 Lacan writes (*The Four Fundamental Concepts of Psycho-Analysis*, p. 106): 'the gaze is the instrument which light is embodied and through which . . . I am photographed.' Lacan's statement is an illustration of how the viewer is never the

centre of vision (the subject is never centred or transcendent), but rather is picture, looked at by others from all directions. This issue is addressed more fully in the second half of my article.

40 Nadar addresses this in his discussion of Balzac and the daguerreotype. 'According to Balzac's theory, all physical bodies are made up entirely of layers of ghostlike images, an infinite number of leaflike skins laid one on top of the other. Since Balzac believed man was incapable of making something material from an apparition, from something impalpable – that is, creating something from nothing – he concluded that every time someone had his photograph taken, one of the spectral layers was removed from the body and transferred to the photograph. Repeated exposures entailed the unavoidable loss of subsequent ghostly layers, that is, the very essence of life' (Nadar, 'My life as a photographer,' trans. Thomas Repensek, *October* 5 (Summer 1978): 9).

41 Luce Irigaray, 'The invisible of the flesh: a reading of Merleau-Ponty, *The Visible and the Invisible*, "The intertwining – the chiasm"', in *An Ethics of Sexual Difference*, trans. Carolyn Burke and Gillian C. Gill (Ithaca, NY: Cornell University Press, 1993), p. 174. Originally published as *Éthique de la différence sexuelle* (Paris: Les Éditions de Minuit, 1984).

42 Susan Rubin Suleiman, *Subversive Intent: Gender, Politics, and the Avant-Garde* (Cambridge: Harvard University Press, 1990), p. 106.

43 John Berger, *Ways of Seeing*, p. 47. Berger's exact words are: '*Men act* and *women appear*. Men look at women. Women watch themselves being looked at. This determines not only most relations between men and women but also the relation of women to themselves. The surveyor of woman in herself is male: the surveyed female. Thus she turns herself into an object – and most particularly an object of vision: a sight.'

44 As Irigaray has argued: 'Investment in the look is not privileged in women as in men. More than the other senses, the eye objectifies and masters. It sets at a distance, maintains the distance. In our culture, the predominance of the look over smell, taste, touch, hearing has brought an impoverishment of bodily relations. It has contributed to disembodying sexuality. The moment the look dominates, the body loses its materiality' (Luce Irigaray, from an interview in *Les Femmes, la pornographie et l'erotisme*, ed. M-F. Hans and G. Lapouge, as quoted in Griselda Pollock, *Vision and Difference* (London and New York: Routledge, 1988), p. 50).

45 Johannes Fabian, *Time and the Other* (New York: Columbia University Press, 1983), p. 106.

46 D-M. Bourneville and P. Régnard, *Iconographie Photographique de la Salpêtrière*, 3 vols (Paris: V. Adrien Delahaye, 1876–80), vol. III (1880), p. 19. Bourneville and Régnard, who were colleagues of Charcot, wrote the following about 'W': '*Durant les attaques, nous avons tracé sur la poitrine, avec la pointe d'une épingle, le nom de la malade et sur le ventre, le mot Salpêtrière*.' 'W' has been identified as Blanche Wittman, the 'Queen of Hysterics', mentioned above. See Owen, *Hysteria, Hypnosis and Healing*, p. 186.

47 Jane Gallop, *The Daughter's Seduction: Feminism and Psychoanalysis* (Ithaca, New York: Cornell University Press, 1982), p. 26.
48 Freud, *Civilization and its Discontents*, p. 99, and Gallop, *The Daughter's Seduction*, p. 27.
49 Freud, *Civilization and its Discontents*, p. 100.
50 Ibid.
51 Gallop, *The Daughter's Seduction*, p. 27.
52 Freud, *Civilization and its Discontents*, p. 106. Freud repeatedly uses this phrase ('*inter urinas et faeces nascimur*') with his commentary on the relationship between neurosis and smell. See, for example, *Dora: An Analysis of a Case of Hysteria* (1905), *Standard Edition*, vol. 7, p. 31, or 'Freud and fetishism: previously unpublished minutes of the Vienna Psychoanalytic Society', p. 159.
53 Freud, *The Complete Letters of Sigmund Freud to Wilhelm Fliess: 1897–1904*, 'Letter of 14.11.97', trans. and ed. Jeffrey Moussaieff Mason (Cambridge: The Belknap Press of Harvard University Press, 1985), p. 280.
54 See especially Freud's 'The instinctual life of obsessional neurotics, and the origins of compulsion and doubt', from *Notes Upon a Case of Obsessional Neurosis, Standard Edition* ('Rat Man', 1909), vol. x, pp. 237–57. The following passage is particularly illustrative (*Notes Upon a Case of Obsessional Neurosis*, p. 237):

> I should like to go back once more to the instinctual life of obsessional neurotics and add one more remark upon it. It turned out that our patient, besides all his other characteristics, was a *renifleur*. By his own account, when he was a child he had recognized every one by their smell, like a dog; and even when he was grown up he was more susceptible to sensations of smell than most people. I have met with the same characteristic in other neurotics, both in hysterical and in obsessional patients, and I have come to recognize that a tendency to taking pleasure in smell, which has become extinct since childhood, may play a part in the genesis of neurosis. And here I should like to raise the general question whether the atrophy of the sense of smell (which was an inevitable result of man's assumption of an erect posture) and the consequent organic repression of his pleasure in smell may not have had a considerable share in the origin of his susceptibility to nervous disease.

55 Freud, *Three Essays on the Theory of Sexuality* (1905), *Standard Edition*, vol. 7, p. 155.
56 Freud, *Fragment of An Analysis of a Case of Hysteria* (Dora, 1905), *Standard Edition*, vol. 7, p. 31.
57 Freud, 'Miss Lucy R (Case 3)' can be found in Josef Breuer and Sigmund Freud, *Studies on Hysteria* (1893–5), *Standard Edition*, vol. 2, pp. 106–24.
58 Freud, *The Complete Letters*, 'Letter of 14.11.97', p. 279.
59 Havelock Ellis, *Studies in the Psychology of Sex, Volume IV, Sexual Selection in Man* (Philadelphia: F. A. Davis Company, 1928), pp. 44–112. The other chapters are devoted to the other senses: 'Touch', 'Hearing', 'Vision'.

60 Ibid., p. 61.
61 Ibid., p. 97.
62 Ibid. For some excellent examples, see pp. 60, 97–8, 107.
63 Alain Corbin, *The Foul and the Fragrant* (New York: Berg, 1986), p. 74.
64 Lacan's most comprehensive discussion of the gaze as *objet petit a* can be found in his *The Four Fundamental Concepts of Psycho-analysis*; see chapters 6–9 under the title 'Of the gaze as *objet petit a*', pp. 67–119.

Despite film theory's focus on the gaze, it has almost overlooked Lacan's own useful theory of the gaze. Joan Copjec writes:

> Film theory introduced the subject into its study, and thereby incorporated Lacanian psychoanalysis, primarily by the means of 'The Mirror Stage as Formative of the Function of the "I."' It is to this essay that theorists made reference as they formulated their arguments about the subject's narcissistic relation to the film and about that relationship's dependence on 'the gaze.' While it is true that the mirror phase essay does describe the child's narcissistic relation to its mirror image, it is *not* in this essay but in Seminar XI that Lacan himself formulates *his* concept of the gaze. Here, particularly in those sessions collected under the heading 'Of the Gaze as *objet petit a*,' Lacan *reformulates* his earlier mirror phase essay and paints a picture very different from the one painted by film theory.
>
> ('The orthopsychic subject: film theory and the reception of Lacan', *October*, no. 49 (Summer 1989): 67–8)

65 The problem of the little 'a' merits some further discussion here. In the space of the *objet petit a*, the little 'a' is meant to stand in for the other (*autre*) as differentiated from, while still referring to the capitalized Other (*Autre* or grand *Autre*). 'However, Lacan refuses to comment on either term here [*objet petit a* or *Autre*], leaving the reader to develop an appreciation of the concepts in the course of their use' (Alan Sheridan in his notes to *The Four Fundamental Concepts of Psycho-analysis*, p. 282). Appreciation is an interesting choice of words here. In any case, I like to think of the desire that is produced and released by the movement of the *objet petit a* as a kind of everyday desire with a little 'd' as differentiated from, while still referring to, Lacan's unnameable and asymptotic Desire for the Real.
66 Lacan, *Television*, trans. Denis Hollier, Rosalind Krauss and Annette Michelson (New York: Norton, 1990), p. 23.
67 Jane Gallop writes, 'The structure [of the *objet petit a*] is analogous to Freud's mechanics of the fetish object' (*The Daughter's Seduction*, p. 40). I think that this is an accurate reading. However, it seems that Catherine Clément lets the two terms come too close when she says that the *objet petit a* is a 'fetish in short'.
68 Lacan, 'Seminar on "The Purloined Letter"', trans. Jeffrey Mehlhman, *Yale French Studies*, 48 (1972): 61 and 63. Originally published in French as '*Le Séminaire sur la Lettre volée*' (1956) and collected in the French edition (and not the English translation) of *Ecrits* (Paris: Editions du Seuil, 1966).

69 Lacan, 'Seminar on "The Purloined Letter"', p. 66.
70 Ibid., p. 66.
71 Ibid.
72 Catherine Clément, *The Lives and Legends of Jacques Lacan*, trans. Arthur Goldhammer (New York: Columbia University Press), p. 192.
73 Ibid., pp. 192–3.
74 Lacan, *The Four Fundamental Concepts of Psycho-analysis*, p. 96.
75 Ibid., p. 95.
76 Ibid., p. 96.
77 Ibid.
78 Ibid., p. 72
79 Norman Bryson, 'The gaze in the expanded field', in *Vision and Visuality*, ed. Hal Foster (Seattle: Bay Press, 1988), p. 93.
80 Clément categorizes the chapters on 'The gaze as *objet petit a*' as a republication of the piece on 'woman-scent' ('Seminar on "The Purloined Letter"'). Clément, *The Lives and Legends of Jacques Lacan*, p. 192.
81 Lacan, *The Four Fundamental Concepts of Psycho-analysis*, pp. 88 and 92.
82 Ibid., p. 82.
83 Ibid., p. 84; emphasis added.
84 Page duBois, *Sowing the Body: Psychoanalysis and Ancient Representations of Women* (Chicago: University of Chicago Press, 1988), p. 188.
85 Michèle Montrelay, 'Inquiry into femininity', *m/f*, 1 (1978). First published in French as 'Recherches sur la féminité', *Critique* (July 1970): 278. For an excellent discussion of Montrelay's use of the phrase '*odor di femina*' see Gallop, *The Daughter's Seduction*, pp. 27–8 and 31–2.
86 Proust describing the taste and smell of the madeleine, *Remembrance of Things Past*, trans, C. K. Scott Moncrieff and Terence Kilmartin (New York: Vintage Books, 1982), vol. 1, p. 51.
87 Lacan, *The Four Fundamental Concepts of Psycho-analysis*, p. 103.
88 Barthes uses the phrase, 'the texture of perfume', to describe the voice of Proust. See 'Odors', in *Roland Barthes by Roland Barthes*, p. 135.

Timothy Mitchell

FIXING THE ECONOMY

Abstract

'Fixing the Economy', shows how the modern understanding of 'the economy' as the totality of the relations of production, distribution and consumption of goods and services within a given country or region arose in a mid-twentieth-century crisis of economic representation. The economy, represented as an autonomous domain, participated in the (largely post-Second World War) re-imagining of the nation-state and the postcolonial international order, and provided a concept of development without political upheaval. In considering the economic life of an Egyptian village, however, Mitchell demonstrates that market and domestic production and consumption are irreducibly hybrid and that the practical foundations of the economy as representation make it impossible any longer to see its imagined referent as the very type of the non-discursive and the material.

Keywords economy; economics; state; Keynes; representation; Egypt; agriculture; households; water buffalo

B`ERAT IS NOT A TYPICAL VILLAGE. It stands across the Nile from Luxor and tourist buses going to Tutankhamun's tomb pass through its outer hamlets. One of these hamlets was built in 1947 by the neo-traditional architect Hasan Fathi, as the first and only part of an unsuccessful programme to rebuild every village in Egypt in a *faux*-traditional Nubian style. The villagers who were to be forcibly relocated there sabotaged its completion. In the 1960s another hamlet grew up adjacent to the temple of Ramses III, housing local families hired as archaeological labourers by the Metropolitan Museum of New York. This hamlet is the setting of the book *Shahhat, an Egyptian* (Critchfield, 1978), a bestselling account by an American journalist of life in the Third World village. The book's realism in portraying the lives of the modernizing poor was praised in the scholarly journals and celebrated by the *New York Times* for making the village of B`erat 'a metaphor for Egypt'.

I have written elsewhere about the manufacture of this kind of realism (Mitchell, 1990, 1991a). The book's realism is constructed by omitting from the picture the tourist industry, the archaeologists, and any sense of the recent history of the place or of the author's own presence in and relationship to the village. The realism is enhanced by the book's frequent use of passages plagiarized from old, out-of-print studies of the Egyptian peasant. The physical description of Shahhat, the book's protagonist, is patched together from the catalogue of 'racial types' in a 1938 study of *The Egyptian Peasant*. The description of the house in which the author, Richard Critchfield, stayed when visiting the village is borrowed from the account of 'Houses of the Lower Orders' in Edward Lane's *Manners and Customs of the Modern Egyptians*, published in 1836. Richard Critchfield was supported by Ford and Rockefeller grants, became a consultant to the US Agency for International Development, and in 1981 was named one of the first recipients of the MacArthur Foundation 'genius' awards for the outstanding intelligence and originality of his work.

It is fairly simple to dismantle this kind of representation of the village, but more difficult to provide an alternative. Part of the problem is that the families of B`erat are themselves caught up in these forms of representation – although only at the margins. The archaeological and tourist industries prescribe that the village stage itself as a traditional place. The government antiquities authority restricts the spread of building in B`erat and stipulates, not always successfully, the use of mud brick in all village architecture. Families that make money from tourism and decide to replace their mud-brick houses with stronger concrete structures must leave the exterior walls intact, raising the concrete pillars and platforms inside the old mud skin.

Shahhat himself made some money for a year or two selling copies of Critchfield's book to tourists at the Colossi of Memnon, before returning to his winter job as a labourer and foreman on French archaeological expeditions. Dozens of other men from the village work in the archeological and tourist industries, as archaeological labourers, hotel and cruise ship employees, guards and petty officials, and small entrepreneurs selling souvenirs. A couple of households own tourist taxis, and three or four families run budget-class local hotels. But it is now illegal to build hotels in the village, and those that already exist seldom have guests.

The tourist industry relies upon the picturesque panorama of the village, but is organized as far as possible to exclude local people from contact with tourists and from the income derived from them. Most tourists to Upper Egypt are accommodated on floating hotels that cruise the Nile between Luxor and Aswan, delivering the tourists directly to archaeological sites along the route and isolating them from all except the most fleeting contact with the local population. The hotel fleets are operated by international hotel chains, who also run five-star hotels in Luxor and Aswan, or by large Egyptian entrepreneurs. Local residents are restricted largely to providing the wage labour required by these enterprises, at subsistence wages.

A fuller picture of B'erat must include the agricultural economy, in which most villagers are employed – but again only at the margins – in activities that can escape adequate representation. The major industry of the village is sugar cane production, but this is dominated by a handful of large farmers. Most of the village's two thousand households survive by operating partly outside this economy, supplementing their incomes from wage labour or small plots of sugar cane with subsistence farming: raising domestic animals and growing small amounts of wheat and other basic crops. This household-based production is not monetarized or accurately recorded, so much of it goes unrepresented in the calculations of the national economy. Just as they are kept out of the picture of the tourist industry, the villagers live on the margins of the nationally and internationally articulated agricultural economy. To make sense of this situation, one has to consider how the national economy, no less than Critchfield's book or the mud-brick houses of the tourist industry, is something fixed – yet never properly fixed – as a representation.

The economy is a concept that seems to resist analysis. It appears to have escaped the kind of critique that now disturbs so many other concepts of modern social theory. The nation can now be seen as something imagined, the state as an indeterminate political project, the public sphere as a structure of exclusion, and class, ethnicity and gender as contingent and unstable constructions. It is unclear why the concept of the economy has not been placed in question in the same way. Perhaps it is assumed to be a much older and somehow more basic term than the other, mostly nineteenth-century constructs. Perhaps the term seems more basic because it is still thought to refer to a material substrate, a realm with an existence prior to and separate from its representations, and thus to stand in opposition to the more discursive constructs of social theory.

Yet these assumptions have no basis. Far from being older than modern social theory, the concept of the economy is much younger. In the sense of the term we now take for granted, referring to the structure or totality of relations of production, distribution and consumption of goods and services within a given country or region, its usage dates only from the mid-twentieth century. Both in academic discourse and in popular expression ('the Egyptian economy', 'the economy is a mess'), this meaning of the term emerged during the years around the Second World War. Adam Smith, dubiously claimed as the father of modern economics, never once refers in *The Wealth of Nations* to a structure or whole of this sort. When he uses the term 'economy', the word carries the older meaning of frugality or the prudent use of resources:

> Capital has been silently and gradually accumulated by the private frugality and good conduct of individuals. . . . It is the highest impertinence and

> presumption . . . in kings and ministers, to pretend to watch over the economy of private people.
>
> (Smith, 1950 [1776]: 327–8)

As recently as the 1920s, the second edition of *Palgrave's Dictionary of Political Economy* contained no separate entry for or definition of the term economy. It used the word only to mean 'the principle of seeking to attain, or the method of attaining, a desired end with the least possible expenditure of means' (Palgrave, 1925–6: 678). In 1932, Lionel Robbins' classic *Essay on the Nature and Significance of Economic Science* described 'The Subject-Matter of Economics' (Chapter 1) as 'human behaviour conceived as a relationship between ends and means' (p.21) and never employed the term 'economy' in its broad contemporary sense.

To trace the appearance of the idea that the economy exists as a general structure of economic relations, the obvious place to begin would be in 1936 with the publication of John Maynard Keynes' *The General Theory of Employment, Interest and Money*. Although tending to use phrases like 'economic society' or 'the economic system as a whole' where today one would simply say 'the economy', *The General Theory* conventionally marks the origin of what came to be called macro-economics. The significance of Keynes is easy to exaggerate, however. Keynes himself was critical of what was arguably a more important development of the 1930s: the birth of econometrics, or the attempt to create a mathematical representation of the entire economic process as a self-contained and dynamic mechanism.

To understand the shift that occurred in the 1930s it will help to look back briefly at the period since the 1870s, when professional, academic economics emerged by making a break with the tradition of political economy from Smith and Ricardo to Marx. The break in the 1870s is usually described in terms of the birth of marginal utility theory – the analysis of economic phenomena as the interaction of buyers and sellers seeking to maximize their individual values or utilities. But the new field marked out by the idea of marginal utility was not the space we know today as the economy. To understand the field of marginal utility, and its transformation in the 1930s, one must first understand its relation not to political economy but to physics.

Physics emerged as a coherent scientific discipline during the second half of the nineteenth century, unified by the new idea of energy. The diversity of what had seemed to be different types of matter associated with heat, light, mechanical force and electricity, each appearing to involve different forces of attraction and repulsion, was replaced by the singular concept of energy, imagined as the unique, protean, yet basically unknowable force at work in all physical processes.

As Philip Mirowski (1988) has shown, scientific economics was created in the 1870s by translating the new language and imagery of physics into a vocabulary and set of metaphors for imagining the field of economic processes. The terminology of the new discipline – words like equilibrium, stability, elasticity, inflation, expansion, contraction, distribution, movement, friction – was borrowed intact from physics. And the central concept of economics, individual utility, was modelled directly on the new idea of energy. It represented the same unique, protean, unknowable force, giving the elements of the economic field their animation.

Economics also borrowed from physics its models of explanation, in particular the prescription to express causal relations in mathematical form. The fact that the central concept of both disciplines was conceived as an invisible and unknowable force encouraged this tendency. This in turn encouraged a predisposition to substitute mathematical description and quantitative measurement for an analysis of the actual nature of the phenomena being described, and to accept such description as a form of proof (Mirowski, 1988: 17). (Despite the aping, a big problem: the law of conservation of energy in physics – the principle that made it possible to constitute diverse phenomena as a single field – had no parallel in economics, creating a fundamental contradiction in the mathematics of the new science. When mathematicians pointed out to economists the basic flaw in their mathematics, the economists told them not to be so picky – while continuing to berate non-mathematical economists for their lack of scientific precision: see Mirowski, 1988: Chapter 2.)

At the same time, professional economists continued to imagine mechanical analogies for the functioning of economic processes. Irving Fisher's 1892 doctoral dissertation, which Paul Samuelson called 'the best of all doctoral dissertations in economics' (Samuelson, 1950: 254, cited Mirowski, 1988: 31), developed a mechanical model of an economic market consisting of a network of cisterns, levers, pipes, rods, sliding pivots and stoppers, through which the flow of water represented the working of the principle of utility. In 1892 he built a working model of this contraption which he used in his classes at Yale for years, until it wore out, and in 1925 he replaced it with an improved model. Fisher argued that the model provided not just a picture of the market but an instrument of investigation, and that the effect of complex variations in the market could be studied by altering the positions of the various stoppers, levers and pivots (Fisher, 1925: iii, 44).

The work of economists like Fisher was the precursor of the emergence of the field of econometrics in the 1930s, through the work of scholars such as the Norwegian Ragnar Frisch and the Dutch scholar Jan Tinbergen. Like their predecessors, these scholars imagined and modelled the economic process as a mechanical apparatus. Frisch, for example, developed a complex mechanical analogy consisting of a small pipe attached to a pendulum suspended beneath a bowl of water, the pipe ending in a valve whose operation depended on the direction of the pendulum's swing (Frisch, 1933: 203–4). Tinbergen actually trained as a physicist before taking up economics.

The transformation in the 1930s marked by the founding of econometrics was understood at the time not, as I am proposing, in terms of the birth of the idea of the economy but as a shift from a static conception of economic processes to a dynamic one. (Even to those looking back after the Second World War, for example, Schumpeter in his *History of Economic Analysis*, it was this rather than Keynesianism that appeared as the major development of the interwar period.) However many rods, levers and stoppers could be made to move in Fisher's model of the market, these represented discrete movements within what was largely a stationary apparatus. What if the apparatus as a whole could be thought to move? What if, as Frisch asked, 'certain exterior impulses hit the economic mechanism and thereby initiate more or less regular oscillations'? (Frisch, 1933: 171). To conceive, however, of the kinds of 'external' forces that would produce a dynamic impulse affecting the entire economic machinery requires two related conceptual shifts. First, a clear distinction has to be elaborated between what Frisch calls 'the intrinsic structure' of the mechanism and its exterior. Second, this intrinsic structure can no longer be imagined as a single market, with a limited number of buyers, sellers and commodities. As a dynamic whole, it must now be thought of as 'the whole economic system taken in its entirety' (p. 172). The reworking of the mechanical imagery in the 1930s to imagine the possibility of an external force creating an impulse that reverberates through and sets up oscillations within a completely closed system marks the birth of the idea of the economy.

Replacing the study of business cycles, in which fluctuations in the price of a single commodity (usually wheat) were correlated with a non-economic cause (usually the weather, or sunspots, or the position of Venus), econometrics tried to construct representations correlating 'every change in economic life'.

The first dynamic model claiming to represent an entire economy was published in 1936, the same year as Keynes' *The General Theory*, by the Dutch economist Jan Tinbergen – who was later to share the first Nobel Prize in economics for this work. In 1939, working for the League of Nations, he produced the first large-scale model of the US economy (Morgan, 1990: 101–30). He had initially trained as a physicist.

> We may start from the proposition that every change in economic life has a number of proximate causes. These proximate causes themselves have their own proximate causes which in turn are indirect 'deeper' causes with respect to the first mentioned change, and so on. Thus a network of causal relations can be laid out connecting up all the successive changes occurring in an economic community.
>
> (Tinbergen, 1937: 8; cited in Morgan, 1990: 103)

As in *The General Theory*, phrases like 'economic life' and 'economic community' express the new idea of the network of relations that would come to be termed the economy.

The economy was formed as a new discursive object in the context of broader developments. Tinbergen developed his first econometric model in response to a Dutch government request for policies to combat the depression (Morgan, 1990: 102). Keynesian theory was also a response to the experience of mass unemployment and depression and to the emergence of New Deal, fascist and other general economic programmes that addressed not just individual human behaviour but the interaction of aggregate and structural factors such as employment, investment and money supply. Also important was the emergence after the First World War of welfare and development programmes for European colonies (Keynes' first job was in the Revenue, Statistics and Commerce Department of the India Office), in response to the growing threats to colonial rule.

But to place the emergence of the economy in this larger context is not a question of supplying the new discursive object with a non-discursive origin. The larger context was itself a discursive one, for the political crises of the 1920s and 1930s were marked by the collapse of systems of monetary representation and the forms of social order and collective identity dependent upon them. The currencies of Russia, Germany, Austria, Hungary and other European countries were destroyed, mostly in less than a year. Recall Polanyi's (1944: 24) account of these events:

> Nations found themselves separated from their neighbors, as by a chasm, while at the same time the various strata of the population were affected in entirely different and often opposite ways. The intellectual middle class was literally pauperized; financial sharks heaped up revolting fortunes. A factor of incalculable integrating and disintegrating force had entered the scene.

As the crisis spread, Britain (in 1931) and then the United States (in 1933) were forced to abandon the gold standard. The foundation of the international financial order, the belief that bank notes had value because they represented gold, was abandoned. It was as the system of monetary representation began to fall apart and the social orders it underpinned lost their coherence that the notion of the economy as a coherent structure came into circulation.

It seems to have taken at least two decades, from the mid-1930s to the mid-1950s, for the economy to come to be understood as a self-evident totality. Even in the early 1950s, the notion of the economy as the total economic process had to be explained, invoked with awkward phrases like 'the economics of the economy'. This was the expression of Edwin Nourse (1953: 15), first Chairman of the Council of Economic Advisors, a body created by the 1946 Employment Act to institutionalize the role of economic expertise within the White House. The Council had only minor influence over presidential policy making, but great influence in placing the voice of economic expertise at the centre of political discourse. No other academic discipline was represented as a field of knowledge within the executive power, a position that enabled economics to situate itself in the postwar period as the true political science. Nourse's attempt to picture the economy as an integrated whole occurs in a statement laying claim to this role of scientific expertise:

> Economic theorists have done a great deal of work in recent years in the area of private business in analyzing the 'economics of the firm.' Of no less importance is the economics of the economy, that is the total economic process. . . . Passage of the Employment Act not only constituted a formal recognition of the integral character of the economics of the economy, but also set up a specific machinery for dealing with this problem in the spirit of science, with the best tools that economic science can provide, and with trained scientific personnel.
>
> (Nourse, 1953: 15–16)

There is no space here to trace the steady emergence of this idea of 'total process' over two decades. Instead I will mention three aspects of the new totality: how it provided a new way for the nation-state to represent itself, a new representation of the international order, and a novel conception of politics as growth.

The emergent discourse of the economy represented, in the first place, a re-imagination of the nation-state. For orthodox, pre-Keynesian economics the sphere of economic behaviour was the individual market. This was the abstraction in terms of which the relations between costs, utilities and prices were to be analysed. *The General Theory* replaced this abstraction, which had no geographical or political definition, with the 'economic system as a whole', a system whose limits corresponded to geopolitical boundaries. The system was represented in terms of a series of aggregates (production, employment, investment and consumption) and synthetic averages (interest rate, price level, real wage, and so on), whose referent was the geographic space of the nation-state (Radice, 1984: 121). This idea of the national economy was not theorized, as Radice points out, but introduced as a commonsense construct providing the boundaries within which the new averages and aggregates could be measured. Subsequently, the division of economics into the separate fields of macro- and micro-economics inscribed this commonsensical reference in the structure of the discipline, where it remained unnoticed. Thinking of the national economy as simply 'the macro level' provided a substitute for a theoretical analysis of its geopolitical construction.

The development of macro-economics and econometrics was accompanied by the creation of a novel vocabulary and methods in statistics for estimating and representing the new aggregates. Simon Kuznets of the National Bureau of Economic Research systematized a method for estimating the national income, which was published in 1941. Kuznets warned that 'a national total facilitates the ascription of independent significance to that vague entity called the national economy' (Kuznets, 1941: xxvi) – which is precisely what happened. (After the war these calculations were taken up elsewhere. In Egypt, for example, the Fouad 1st

Society of Political Economics began the first efforts to compute the country's national income around 1950 (Badawi, 1951: 6).) The subsequent elaboration of what came to be called the Gross National Product of each economy made it possible to represent the size, structure and growth of this new totality. Thus the development of the economy as a discursive object between the 1930s and the 1950s provided a new language in which the nation-state could speak for itself and imagine its existence as something natural, bounded and subject to political management.

The second aspect of the new discourse of the economy was the re-imagination of the international order. The dissolution of European empires before and after the Second World War disturbed the representation of the world in terms of position in an imperial order. Here too the economy provided a new way of imagining geopolitical space. Previously it made little sense to talk of, say, the British economy, so long as Britain's economic realm was thought to include India and its other colonies. More generally, a world that was pictured as consisting outside Europe of a series of extensive but discontinuous European empires could not easily be imagined to contain a large number of separate economies, each economy coinciding with a self-contained geographical space and consisting of the totality of economic relations within that space.

The collapse of empire and the growing hegemony of the United States created a new order, consolidated first by the League of Nations and then by the UN, the World Bank and the International Monetary Fund, in which the world was pictured in the form of separate nation-states, with each state marking the boundary of a distinct economy. Again, the new macro-economics took these imagined objects as its untheorized referents: international trade was measured in terms of aggregates (imports and exports of goods and capital) and averages (terms of trade, exchange rates) that were defined in terms of the transactions between national economies (Radice, 1984: 121). The UN and the World Bank helped construct the new global imaginary through the publication of statistics and the proliferation of programmes defining as their object these separate economies.

A third aspect of the geospatial representation of the economy was that the new object could be imagined to grow – without altering its physical limits. Mainstream, pre-Keynesian economics did not develop a concern with economic growth. If growth was discussed, it was imagined as a natural process of spatial and material expansion – the opening up of new territories, the growth of new cities, the development of new manufactures and markets, the expansion of trade and, above all, the necessary expansion of population. Because the object of economic discourse was not itself a spatially fixed entity, economic growth was not a problematic question. Once economic discourse took as its object the fixed space of the nation-state – coinciding with the crisis of over-production and stagnation in the 1930s – it became both possible and necessary to imagine economic growth in new terms, not as material and spatial extension but as the internal intensification of the totality of relations defining the economy as an object.

The idea that the economy was an object whose basic characteristic was to grow transformed political language in the postwar period in both the First World and the Third. In the United States, the architects of the cold war seized upon a form of militarization that, for the first time, did not appear to require sacrifices from the civilian population. War, it was said, could be financed by growth. In reference to countries outside the West, 'to develop' ceased to be just a transitive verb (referring to the exploitation of a particular territory or resource) and began to refer to an intransitive political and economic process: development. The prewar concern with colonial welfare was transformed into the postwar ideology of developing what was now called the underdeveloped world (a label that initially shocked Egyptians when they discovered it was to include them (Lackani, 1951)). Urged on by the United States, postcolonial regimes took up the theme of economic growth to organize and represent their relationship to the populations they now governed. Foreign assistance programmes were introduced, graduates were sent to the United States and Europe for training in the new sciences of development, and local departments of economics were set up – although not until 1962 in the case of Cairo University. All these innovations in the name of development took the economy as their object and helped establish it within countries like Egypt as a self-evident structure.

The emergence of the economy, then, should not be examined merely as a conceptual innovation within the discipline of economics or in general social theory. These intellectual developments accompanied and interacted with a broader discursive change in which political and social practice constructed a new object. The economy came into being between the 1930s and 1950s as the field of operation for new powers of planning, regulation, statistical enumeration and representation. Through these novel forms of political rationality and practice it became possible to imagine the economy as a self-contained sphere, distinct from the social, the cultural, and other spheres.

The economy now plays such a powerful role in political discourse it is difficult to imagine that it emerged so recently – that only since the middle third of the twentieth century has it been imagined to exist. If the economy is just a discursive construction, moreover, the question arises why it has become so powerful. If it is a mere representation, why do we not see through it? The problem with the question lies in the word 'mere', for a representation is never, as it always pretends to be, a mere representation. The word implies a more substantial reality hidden beneath or behind the discursive order, a reality unmarked by representation. This is precisely the effect of the modern order of representation, the effect of a world divided into material reality and the mere representations through which we know and organize it (Mitchell, 1988). The construction of the economy is a particularly powerful instance of the production of this effect, for the 'real' economic relations to which economic discourse refers have become the epitome of a material, non-discursive reality.

The power of the economy as a discursive process lies exactly with fixing this effect of the real (economy) versus its representation. The proliferation of models, statistics, plans and programmes of economic discourse all claim to represent the different elements and relationships of a real object, the national economy. Yet this object, as one could show at length, is itself constituted as a discursive process, a phenomenon of values, representations, communications, meanings, goals and uses, none of which can be separated from or said to pre-exist their representation in economic discourse.

The invention of the economy required a great work of imagination on the part of economists and econometricians, to find methods of representing every relationship constituting a nation's economic life and giving each one a value. At the same time, the invention also required a process of exclusion. To fix a self-contained sphere like the economy requires not only methods of counting everything within it, but also, and perhaps more importantly, some method of excluding what does not belong. No whole or totality can be represented without somehow fixing its exterior. To create the economy meant also to create the non-economic.

Two aspects of what came to be excluded as standing outside the sphere of the economy deserve to be mentioned: the state and the household. The state presents itself as the site of the modes of planning and regulation that take the economy as their object. It is also the apparatus principally responsible for constructing representations of the economy, by defining, gathering and publishing economic data. In the form of the nation-state, this same apparatus establishes the spatial boundaries of the economy, creating the currency, the customs barriers and geographical borders that appear to separate one economy from the next. For all these reasons it seems clear that the state stands outside the economy, defining, representing and regulating the entire field of economic relations. Indeed, without these forms of regulation and representation, as one could demonstrate at some length, the economy would not exist.

This raises an obvious problem. If the economy cannot exist apart from its modes of regulation and representation, it is not clear that these modes can be excluded from the definition of the economy. If capital, for example, exists in the form of private property and property can only exist as a certain structure of legal and political relationships, then these relationships are not something outside of and separate from the economy. It is not clear, in other words, that the state does form an exterior, non-economic sphere, defining the limits of the economy. The geopolitical aspect of the state offers another example: the borders of the state do not in fact contain the economy, for economic powers and relations often extend beyond the geographical limit that represents the imaginary space of an economy. The border is just a mode of intervening in and representing certain larger economic relations. Neither the economy nor the state forms a self-contained, free-standing sphere. To put this the other way round, the discursive practices that appear to separate the economy from the state should be grasped not as signs marking the border between two spheres but as powerful organizing practices that create the material effect of the economy as an apparently self-contained structure (cf. Mitchell, 1991b, 1992) – material, in the sense that the everyday force of the political order of capitalism is structured out of these discursive effects.

The second significant sphere defined as non-economic, the household, can be examined in a similar fashion. The economy is a sphere defined to exclude forms of productive activity, exchange and consumption that do not involve the system of money. If you travel to work on foot, the journey is not part of the economy. If you take a bus, your trip becomes part of the economy. Walking, whatever the distance, does not contribute to GNP, but riding a bus does. If you stay at home and do unpaid domestic labour, your work itself is outside the economy. It is a well-studied feature of capitalist economies that the domestic labour of child-rearing, cleaning, washing and preparing meals, done largely by women, is placed outside the system of monetary exchange (e.g. Smith *et al.*, 1984). It constitutes the so-called non-economic sphere of the private household.

The household marks another boundary of the economy, the one where monetary relations cease and the private or family sphere begins. Yet this boundary is as uncertain as that represented by the state. In the first place, the functioning of the economy depends on 'externalizing' the costs of reproducing the labour force, by having domestic labour performed without pay. What is organized and represented as external and secondary is actually central to the continued existence of the monetary economy. This dependence underlies a more general phenomenon. The conception and arrangement of the economy as a self-contained sphere requires from the beginning, and at every point, in every interaction and exchange, the maintaining of a difference between the monetary and non-monetary, the economic and the personal, the public and the private. This process of differentiation, very fuzzy and uncertain in its details, precedes and makes possible the effect of the economy as a self-contained sphere. In this broader sense, then, what is depicted as the non-economic is implicated at every point in the creation of the economy.

In a country such as Egypt, lying towards what we picture as the margins of the world economy, this uncertainty of the distinction between the economic and the non-economic takes on a greater significance, for several reasons. First, the formation and relative strength of the state-capitalist class and the nature of its capital gives a special significance to supposedly non-economic relationships of patronage, nepotism and corruption, so that at the very centres of economic power distinctions between the public and private realm, between the economy and personal wealth, between work and private life, are often likely to be blurred. Second, on the fringes of the economy lies the vast so-called informal sector, the household or neighbourhood-based production and distribution of small-scale goods and services, unregistered with the state and operating outside its system of revenue and regulation, whose activities represent a large but unknown proportion of the country's productive life (Abdel-Fadil, 1983). This sector is traditionally excluded from calculations of GNP and other representations of the economy (although the development industry has recently become interested in penetrating this sphere, in an effort to compensate for the failure of development in the formal sector). Finally, there is the rural phenomenon of household-based agricultural production. With the village of B`erat in mind, it is here that I want to focus.

Despite the global spread of capitalist agriculture, peasant- or household-based agricultural production has survived and shows no sign of disappearing. This has stimulated a long debate, with its origins in discussions of the Russian peasantry but taken up over the last two decades first in African and South Asian Studies and more recently in writing on the Middle East. The research on the Middle East, including Egypt, points to a basic distinction in rural society between the small peasant household, where production is oriented towards subsistence and the reproduction of the household, and capitalist farming integrated into the national and international economy. The work on Egypt by Georg Stauth (1983, 1990) has provided part of the theoretical basis for a proposed new approach to the study of agrarian society in the Middle East, one that does justice to the phenomenon of peasant agriculture and attempts to explain its persistence.

Stauth terms the particular relationship between capitalist farming and subsistence households found in contemporary Egypt the '`izba system', re-employing the term for the large landed estate that developed in Egypt from the mid-nineteenth century. The word referred originally to the housing complex built on the estate for its workforce, who were typically given a small plot to grow food to support themselves while their labour, housing, domestic animals and farm implements remained the property of the estate owner. The agrarian reforms of the 1950s and 1960s broke up these estates, dispossessed the largest, mostly absentee owners, and redistributed the land. Many small farmers benefited from the redistribution, but the biggest beneficiaries were large landowners living in the countryside. They were able to preserve and often enlarge their holdings, usually dividing the title among different family members to avoid the ceiling on ownership while continuing to manage the property as a single farm. In B`erat, for example, about 1300 acres of sugar cane estate were taken over by the state and redistributed in plots of two to three acres to small farmers (although many of these are about to lose the land again, following the 1992 reversal of a central part of the Nasserist land reform programme). Meanwhile, three or four large landowning families within the village bought up or rented land from absentee owners who possessed more than the legal limit of 300 acres (later reduced to fifty acres). By dividing the title among brothers, these families created farms ranging in size from over fifty to several hundred acres.

The effect of these changes, argues Stauth, has been to re-embed the `izba system within the communal structures of the village. Large farms, from five to several hundred acres in size, are organized for production for the market. Smaller holdings are oriented towards subsistence farming, with the smallest owners and the landless supplying the wage labour required by the market-sector farms. In place of the old method of housing and reproducing the labour force within the estate, the market sector now externalizes the process of reproducing its labour force. The costs of reproduction are carried by the subsistence sector, which is dependent for its survival on jobs in the market sector. This new form of the `izba system, says Stauth, keeps the small peasantry alive, providing the mechanism for incorporating their labour into an internationally articulated market economy.

The `izba relationship, according to Stauth, can also explain why apparently traditional social and cultural forms persist within the village – even among the large, capitalist landowning families. Under the `izba system, those who are employed on the large farms do not form an uprooted proletariat, fully integrated into the capitalist economy. Because they sustain and reproduce their lives outside the capitalist sector, they escape the economic discipline and regulation that govern the lives of a capitalist workforce. So the large landowners have to substitute 'non-economic' methods of integrating and regulating the peasantry. They employ political means – the direct coercive control exercised by those who supply and supervise the gangs of wage labourers – but also social and cultural means. The large landowners typically control the village headmanship and the membership of village arbitration committees. They also play a leading role in the village mosques and as the heads of powerful *`a'ilas* (the extended families or clans of which the village is composed). These positions, says Stauth, enable them to interfere in the moral life of the subsistence sector, by maintaining the valuation of kinship ties, associated patterns of deference and obligation, and religious norms of piety and generosity. The 'symbolic and obligatory framework' maintained in this manner prescribes 'the specific boundaries of social practice in the village' and compensates for the failure to integrate the small peasantry into the regulative forms of the capitalist economy (Stauth, 1990: 125, 136).

Glavanis and Glavanis (1983, 1990) draw on the work of Stauth, as well as the earlier contribution of Islamoglu and Keyder (1977) and the broader debate on the articulation of modes of production, to propose a new approach to the study of agrarian society in the Middle East. The aim is to explain the persistence of the peasant or household form of production, without reducing the phenomenon to the stubbornness of tradition or a mere delay in the process of proletarianization driven by the global expansion of capitalism. By taking seriously the subsistence household as a form of production and examining closely the `izba system or other methods of articulation between the household and capitalist sectors, the aim is to uncover the diversity of strategies with which rural populations try to resist or accommodate the penetration of capital. Such an approach, it is hoped, will relocate the principal dynamic of change within rather than outside Middle Eastern societies and enable them to 'recapture their own history' (Glavanis and Glavanis, 1983: 36).

There have been strong objections to this way of looking at agrarian social relations. David Seddon (1986), drawing on the work of Bernstein (1981), argues that trying to help peasants recapture their own history represents an illusory and reactionary form of peasant populism. To focus on the subsistence-oriented peasant household as a form of production, with its own internal logic, assumes that the household sector remains intact as it is incorporated into the wider capitalist system. Its articulation with the capitalist sector is thought of as an external relation. The household-based peasantry is considered to be a single class, without significant internal divisions, and as a class it tries to resist external exploitation. This resistance and survival of the peasantry is given a false analytical priority and historical significance.

Instead, Seddon and Bernstein argue, one should begin the analysis from the point of view of the global development of capitalism and its destruction of what Bernstein (1981: 5) schematically terms the 'natural economy' of the pre-colonial period – meaning an economy dominated by production for subsistence, whatever the degree of marketing of a surplus or its appropriation as tribute. Pre-capitalist forms or units of production are subsumed into the circuit of capital as they become caught up in an increasing dependence on commodities. As the need to produce commodities grows, peasants become subject to the process of capitalist class formation. This happens not only through relations of exchange, but through increasing efforts by the capitalist sector and the state to intervene in the production process in the countryside, setting price controls, creating market monopolies, instituting compulsory cropping, and policing village disputes. The peasant or household sector may remain in immediate control of the organization of production, but its survival or even re-emergence is a consequence, not a determinant, of agrarian change.

Rather than restoring the peasant as a historical actor, says Seddon, we should dissolve the category altogether. There is no distinctive, independent, undivided peasant identity. The position of the small commodity producer in the countryside represents a contradictory unity of the class positions of capital and labour (Seddon, 1986: 167). In other words, the peasant is to be denied a particular historical role of his own, and identified as the local bearer of the global contradiction of capitalism.

Is there a way to go beyond the increasingly familiar terms of this debate? First of all, thanks to works such as Ken Cuno's (1992) study of eighteenth-century rural Egypt, we know that cash-crop agriculture, the commoditization of land and a highly stratified rural society existed in places like the Nile Delta decades, and probably centuries, before the nineteenth-century colonial transformation.

The notion of a precolonial 'natural economy' cannot capture this complex mixture of subsistence and market-oriented agriculture or account for the contribution of local institutions and social forces to the later development of Egyptian capitalism. One does not have to resort to peasant populism to argue that, from the beginning, the emergence of a capitalist world system was dependent on dynamics at work in places that were to become the peripheries of that system.

On the other hand, the attempt to theorize about the persistence within the capitalist system of the apparently non-capitalist peasant household encounters a serious difficulty. The difficulty lies in how to draw the distinction between the capitalist sector and subsistence or household sector. Studies of rural Egypt are never certain at what point small peasants get big enough to be considered capitalists. At first, Stauth (1983: 88–9) seems to define the capitalist sector as landholdings of more than twenty acres. Elsewhere (1990: 139) he defines the subsistence sector as holdings of less than five acres, but adds that even holdings from one to five acres should be excluded from this sector if they employ one or other variation of the `izba system.

Perhaps it would be better to focus on the orientations of the households themselves rather than trying to base the distinction between subsistence and capitalist sectors on different sizes of landholding. But here the distinction becomes even less clear, as one can see if we return to the evidence from the village of B`erat. We can begin there with the gamoosa.

The most common form of subsistence household production in the village is the raising of domestic animals. The majority of small plots that are not committed to sugar cane production are used to grow fodder, in particular for the raising of water buffalo. The buffalo calf is purchased not from accumulated monetary savings, which almost no one has, but by creating an informal savings cooperative (a *gam`iyya*, or rotating credit union) with neighbours and relatives. When the animal is fully grown and can give birth, its calves are sold on the market. Alternatively, they can be kept as a form of savings (a form that, unlike money, cannot be frittered away accidentally or filched by one's husband) and sold when a large sum of cash is needed. In the meantime, milk from the buffalo is consumed directly or processed into cheese, yoghurt, curds and whey, which supply an important part of the household diet. The animal's dung provides fuel for the other major domestic food production, the baking of bread. Larger households, or smaller ones without young children, where women have more labour time available, may raise three or four buffalo and cows and market some of the milk products as well. So the buffalo is simultaneously a means of producing for the market and a means of subsistence. The distinction between market and subsistence sectors runs down the middle of the gamoosa.

If one turns to the major market crop, sugar cane, there are similar difficulties in drawing a line between household and market. Although sugar cane is Egypt's second largest industrial crop, it requires almost no market-purchased inputs. There are no seeds to buy, as the cane stays in the ground for three to five years and is then replanted using ratoons from the last year's crop. It requires no pesticides, little fertilizer, and relatively infrequent irrigation. The one major input, the labour of harvesting, costs almost nothing. Cutting the cane, stripping the leaves and bundling it to be loaded on to carts is often done without payment, by women and older children, in exchange for taking the leaves to use as animal fodder in the household. The cultivator pays only for the labour of loading the cane on to the tractor carts and light-railway trucks that take it to the mill. Thus even the most market-oriented agricultural production contains and depends upon subsistence-oriented labour.

To give another example, the households of B`erat's largest capitalist farmers, owners of several dozen or even hundreds of acres, in most cases differ only in size rather than kind from more subsistence-oriented households. In fact, as they are capable of supplying almost all household food consumption from their own fields, they are more self-supporting and less market-dependent than smaller households. The women of wealthy households still bake bread and raise domestic animals. They do not work in the fields collecting fodder, it is true, but nor do the women of smaller households where circumstances permit.

Numerous other examples could be described that show the difficulty of drawing a distinction between the market sector and the household sector. To put this in the context of our earlier discussion, in B`erat one would find it difficult to determine where the economy ends and the household begins. The economy has no distinct edge. Within the village, the national and transnational discursive regime that attempts to establish the economy as a self-contained sphere and to organize its development seems to lose its definition.

Rereading, in this light, the analysis of scholars like Stauth, one is struck by the neatness with which they divide the Egyptian village into a market sector and a subsistence sector, into what is economic and what is non-economic (or as Stauth puts it, 'cultural' or 'traditional'). This analytical neatness fails to correspond to the uncertainty and ambiguity of relationships in the village, where lives are constructed on the edge of the economy in ways that often seem to escape its terms.

Moreover, the neat categorizations with which this ambiguity is overlooked tend to reiterate the ordered discourse of capitalism itself. This kind of analysis, in other words, is unintentionally complicitous with the discursive order of capital, with its attempt to establish the economy as a distinct, self-contained sphere – a sphere in whose construction the cultural, the traditional, the personal, supposedly play no part, except by their exclusion. All the debates that follow about the `izba relationship, the articulation of the household sector with capitalist economy, the subsumption of subsistence forms of production by the expansion of global capitalism, the insistence that all explanations start from and return to this historical movement of capital, fall within rather than outside the discourse of capitalist modernity. They cannot consider that the lives of a village might somehow not quite fit the categories and identities offered by this history.

The argument of those like Seddon that small peasants embody the contradiction of capital and labour at least acknowledges that their lives escape the singular identities into which capitalist modernity attempts to organize them. But rather than take this hybridism seriously, the argument retains the identities intact as the foundation of the explanation and reduces the villagers themselves to temporary contradictions destined to resolve themselves in the future into one or other of their underlying identities.

The insistence on identities that do not break down and on categories that are self-contained ignores the discursive process of exclusion and differentiation, always incomplete, by which such unities are constructed. Stauth and others point out that the non-economic or subsistence sector in the village depends on the market economy to reproduce itself. At the same time, it should be said, the economic sector depends on the so-called non-economic realm. This is true in the more straightforward sense, as Stauth himself makes clear, that the market sector needs to place outside the market economy the costs of reproducing its labour force. But this dependence coincides with the more general phenomenon addressed in our earlier discussion of economic discourse: the economy must be constructed as a whole, with a boundary that marks its exterior. The boundary is established by excluding what is determined as non-economic. In this more complex sense, too, the economy depends upon the non-economic – and never quite succeeds in excluding it. It is in this contradictory border region of exclusion-yet-dependence that the lives of the villagers of B`erat acquire their indeterminacy.

Instead of extending the debates over the identity of contemporary peasantries, the nature of the non-economic or subsistence sector, and its relationship to the capitalist economy, we should take seriously the phenomenon that small rural households seem to be fixed within the categories of economic discourse. At the limits of the economy the distinctions between economic and non-economic, modern and non-modern, capitalist and non-capitalist, becomes ambiguous. This is not to say that we should celebrate this ambiguity as an act of resistance by a defiant peasantry. That would make the mistake of setting up the peasantry once again as a self-formed historical actor, with an identity outside the origins and spread of capitalism and heroically opposing it. Rather, by looking beyond the discourse of identity, of capitalism and its others, we can consider how the categories of capitalist modernity – in this case the economy – are necessarily incomplete. The categories themselves cannot mark their own edges, and the attempt to create an edge forms a margin of indeterminacy that modernity cannot erase.

Is there a sense, after all, in which we can take the villagers of B`erat as typical of something? Not of the Egyptian peasant, or the Third World poor, or any other determined identity that the tourist brochures and popular books might offer. Rather, recall that even today, a century or more after the global consolidation of the capitalist order, half a century or more after the invention of the economy, a majority of people live hybrid lives, neither market nor subsistence, neither capital nor labour, neither within the national economy nor quite outside it, escaping the fixed categories of economic discourse. The undetermined identities of those whose lives place them at the edge of the economy represent neither a non-economic exterior, nor a temporary contradiction destined to resolve itself.

References

Abdel-Fadil, Mahmoud (1983) 'Informal sector employment in Egypt', in R. Lobbon (ed.) *Urban Research Strategies for Egypt*, Cairo Papers in Social Science, 6(2): 16–40, Cairo: American University in Cairo Press.

Badawi, Helmy Bahgat (1951) Paper delivered to the Fouad 1st Society of Political Economics, February. In United States, Department of State, Egypt, 874.00 TA/2–951, from Cairo to Department of State, 9 February, enclosure 2.

Bernstein, Henry (1981) 'Concepts for the analysis of contemporary peasantries', in Rosemary Galli (ed.) *The Political Economy of Rural Development: Peasants, International Capital, and the State*, Albany: State University of New York Press, pp. 3–24. Reprinted from *Journal of Peasant Studies*, 6(4) (1979).

Critchfield, Richard (1978) *Shahhat: An Egyptian*, Syracuse: Syracuse University Press. Cairo edition: American University in Cairo Press, 1982.

Cuno, Kenneth M. (1992) *The Pasha's Peasants: Land, Society, and Economy in Lower Egypt, 1740–1858*, Cambridge: Cambridge University Press.

Girard, P. S. (1821–9) 'Mémoire sur l'agriculture, l'industrie et le commerce de l'Egypte', *Description de l'Egypte*, vol. 17, Paris.

Glavanis, Kathy and Glavanis, Pandeli (1983) 'The sociology of agrarian relations in the Middle East: the persistence of household production', *Current Sociology*, 31(2): 1–110.

—— (eds) (1990) *The Rural Middle East: Peasant Lives and Modes of Production*, Ramallah: Bir Zeit University, and London: Zed Press.

Islamoglu, Huri and Keyder, Caglar (1977) 'Agenda for Ottoman history', *Review*, 1(1): 31–55.

Keynes, John Maynard (1936) *The General Theory of Employment, Interest and Money*, London.

Kuznets, Simon (1941) *National Income and Its Composition, 1919–1939*, vol. 1, New York: National Bureau of Economic Research.

Lackany, S. (1951) 'Point IV: its role in fostering private investment', in United States, Department of State, Egypt, 874.00 TA/2–951, from Cairo to Department of State, 9 February, enclosure 1.

Lawson, Fred H. (1981) 'Rural revolt and provincial society in Egypt, 1820–1824', *International Journal of Middle East Studies*, 13.

Mitchell, Timothy (1988) *Colonising Egypt*, Cambridge: Cambridge University Press.

—— (1990) 'The invention and re-invention of the Egyptian peasant', *International Journal of Middle East Studies*, 22(2) (May): 129–50.

—— (1991a) 'A reply to Richard Critchfield', *International Journal of Middle East Studies*, 23(2) (May): 279–80.

—— (1991b) 'The limits of the state: beyond statist approaches and their critics', *American Political Science Review*, 85: 77–96.

—— (1992) 'Going beyond the state? A response to critiques', *American Political Science Review*, 86.

Morgan, Mary S. (1990) *The History of Econometric Ideas*, Cambridge: Cambridge University Press.

Nourse, Edwin G. (1953) *Economics in the Public Service*, New York: Harcourt, Brace.

Palgrave, Robert Harry Inglis (ed.) (1925–6) *Palgrave's Dictionary of Political Economy* (2nd edn.), London: Macmillan.

Polanyi, Karl (1944) *The Great Transformation*, New York: Rinehart & Co.

Radice, Hugo (1984) 'The national economy: a Keynesian myth?', *Capital and Class*, 22: 111–40.

Robbins, Lionel (1935) *An Essay on the Nature and Significance of Economic Science* (2nd edn.) (1st edn. 1932), London: Macmillan.

St John, J. A. (1845) *Egypt and Nubia, Their Scenery and their People*, London.

Seddon, David (1986) 'Commentary on agrarian relations in the Middle East: a "new paradigm" for analysis?', *Current Sociology*, 34(2): 151–72.

Smith, Adam (1950) (1776) *An Enquiry into the Nature and Causes of the Wealth of Nations*, London: Methuen.

Smith, Joan, Wallerstein, Immanuel and Evers, Hans-Dieter (eds) (1984) *Households and the World Economy*, Beverly Hills, CA: Sage Publications.

Stauth, Georg (1983) *Die Fellachen im Nildelta: Zur Struktur des Konflikts zwischen subsistenz- und warenproduktion in Ländlichen Ägypten*, Wiesbaden: Franz Steiner.

—— (1990) 'Capitalist farming and small peasant households in Egypt', in Glavanis and Glavanis (1990), pp. 122–41. Reprinted from *Review*, 7(2) (1983): 285–314.

Tinbergen, Jan (1937) *An Econometric Approach to Business Cycle Problems*, Paris: Hermann & Cie.

Aleks Sierz

CULTURAL POLICY AND THE CRITICAL INTELLECTUAL

Jim McGuigan, *Culture and the Public Sphere* (London: Routledge, 1996) 220 pp., ISBN 0-415-11262-1 £45.00 Hbk; ISBN 0-415-11263-X £13.99 Pbk.

After tackling cultural populism in 1992, Jim McGuigan now turns his attention to a subject every bit as wide-ranging: what does cultural studies have to say about cultural policy? Starting with a brief account of 'cultural policy studies' – whose project is to 'forge a much stronger relationship' between cultural studies and cultural policy (p. 5) – he argues that 'issues of cultural policy may usefully be considered from the point of view of a critical and communicative rationality' (p. 1). In other words, how can Habermas help us to make sense of cultural policy?

After a friendly tussle with Australian cultural policy studies – Tony Bennett, Ian Hunter, Stuart Cunningham and Tom O'Regan – McGuigan starts with an ambitious attempt to persuade policy-makers that instrumental reason is not enough. Instead of seeing cultural policy as simply a question of arts management, his perspective is that it is an example of cultural politics in the widest sense. As such, it can be better understood by means of critical reason. Enter Habermas, Foucault and Bourdieu.

In the main body of the book, McGuigan opts for a 'multiperspectival approach', which he uses to discuss 'the function of public debate' (p. 29) in a number of key areas. There follow chapters on questions of value, state subsidy, cultural industries, urban regeneration, national heritage, racial identity and censorship. The examples discussed include the American culture wars, the Keats versus Dylan fracas, the rise of market forces in the BBC and Arts Council, the GLC's arts policies, the LA riots and the culture of contentment, the UK's heritage industry, the uses of cultural hybridity, the manufacture of consent, and the issue of whether the media need a moral code.

Well-written, serious and accessible, *Culture and the Public Sphere* is right up to date with its examples of cultural debate. It covers postmodernism's effect on the distinction between high and low culture, the effect of business ideology in public arts administration, the post-Fordist restructuring of the cultural industries, the problems of decayed inner cities, heritage tourism, cultural citizenship, panopticism and the question of moral regulation, especially of children's media consumption.

Students will find these chapters a very useful summary of public debates and will surely appreciate McGuigan's clarity, fair-mindedness and ability to report arguments concisely. But if each chapter is a neat essay, collectively they are something of a disappointment. Although his use of Habermas or Foucault can be momentarily illuminating, he never applies their ideas systematically. Given his ambitious scope, it is also disappointing that his examples are not linked by any forceful argument. The use of a 'multiperspectival approach' – and his disclaimer that 'these studies represent no grand theoretical plan' (p. 177) – results in a lack of focus.

While McGuigan's idea of the public sphere is certainly a wide one, the examples he quotes are from a narrow range of sources, mainly academic. While the public debate is conducted on television, radio and in the newspapers, McGuigan uses textbook summaries rather than primary sources. He doesn't ask what the audience watching the debate thinks, nor what its wider social effects are.

In Chapter 2, for example, McGuigan argues – quite rightly – that even in an era of postmodernity, where cultural boundaries tend to blur and cultural hierarchies are prone to collapse, there is still a need for value judgements. Yet this large and important subject is handled in a wide-ranging but rather inconclusive way. He stresses the role of ethical considerations in discussions of cultural value, but his conclusion – cultural conditions are 'perpetually being put in question' by the 'culture of dissatisfaction' (p. 50) – is a bit lame.

Another disappointment is that while the cover of the book – I. M. Pei's pyramid outside the Louvre – suggests a European perspective, most of McGuigan's examples hail from Britain, the USA and Australia. Jack Lang only gets two mentions; the European Union scarcely more.

By the last chapter it is clear that McGuigan is less interested in culture and the public sphere than in criticism and the role of the intellectual. Arguing that 'questions of cultural policy are too important to be left solely to cultural technicians' (p. 188), he makes a plea for greater use of critical reason. Criticism is assumed to be good for you, but *how* it could help policy-makers is never shown. Would a dose of Habermas make their policies better – or just expand their worldview? McGuigan doesn't say. Nor does he explain why the gulf between cultural studies and cultural policy is such a bad thing.

For McGuigan, critical practice means human emancipation – and the world is neatly split into *techne* ('instrumental rationality's mode of practicality') and *praxis* (yes, 'communicative rationality's mode of practicality'). But seeing cultural policy-makers as those 'who want recipe knowledge, but not critical thought, information but not ideas' (p. 187) sounds like special pleading. If arts administrators find such comments insulting, they may be amused to learn that 'not everyone employed in intellectual work can be a Chomsky, a Sartre or a Said' (p. 186). Indeed.

At the end, McGuigan not only leaves an open answer to Douglas Kellner's self-regarding question: 'How can critical intellectuals be practical?', but he also adds a question of his own: 'How can practical intellectuals be critical?' (p. 190). The result is that the reader closes the book exasperated by a sudden glimpse of intellectuals chasing their own tails.

Marcia Landy

SURVEYING THE BORDERS OF BRITISH CINEMATIC CULTURE

Sarah Street, *British National Cinema* (London: Routledge, 1997) 232 pp., ISBN 0-415-06735-9 £45.00 Hbk; ISBN 0-415-06736-7 £12.99 Pbk.

Sarah Street's *British National Cinema* is a complex, multifaceted, and even ironic treatment of cherished assumptions and judgements about British cinematic culture. Street draws on a number of sources to document her carefully considered treatment of British cinema from its inception as the 'last machine of Victorian invention' to the present moment of new visual and informational technologies. In assessing the uncertain future of the British film industry, she notes ironically 'that the production sector has practically returned to its original cottage-industry structure' (p. 23). Her examination of British film production entails a detailed analysis of the fiscal and cultural politics of film that have spawned an 'official' and 'unofficial' cinema. Unlike many treatments of British cinema that have tended to be melodramatic about its failure in economic and cultural terms, or to prescribe a direction (quality, anti-Americanism, or realism) for the medium, or have focused on specialized aspects of British film production – censorship, studios, genres, stars, directors, forms of acting, formal textual analysis, themes, or linear histories – Street's book adopts an eclectic examination exploring exemplary moments in British history and cinema history: the rise, transformation and fall of certain dominant genres (e.g. comedy, melodrama, social problem films, among others), their association with particular stars and studios, the existence of a 'modernist' and 'counter cinema', and the rise of new aesthetic and political movements that are challenging British national culture.

In particular, Street's discussion of British stardom (often disclaimed as a crucial factor in British film production) is exemplary for the ways it situates the relationship between British acting styles in the theatre and cinema and for its carefully reasoned and differentiated analysis of star qualities and their role in the national imaginary. Since Jessie Matthews and Gracie Fields have been more extensively considered as national icons, Street focuses on the figure of Anna Neagle to 'assess culturally dominant values and implicit challenges to them' (p. 124). Through her discussion of Neagle, Street identifies qualities germane to British stardom and national consensus in the 1930s and 1940s as well as the waning of 'a comforting sense of Britishness' in the late 1950s and after. Neagle's 'resolutely British, non-European and white identity' conveyed 'individual stoicism in the face of adversity as a means of communicating . . . [an] overall liberal-conservative political ideology' (p. 126). According to Street, this 'English rose . . . epitomised middle class values of thrift, hard work, stoicism, and feminine modesty'. Neagle was identified with historical films through such famous figures as Florence Nightingale and Nurse Edith Cavell, roles that identified the star with nationalist concerns but also featured her as resolute and proto-feminist. As with Street's discussion of directors, studios and genres, her discussion of stars is properly attentive to the certainty that (1) there does exist a popular British cinema; (2) stardom operates within this cinema to communicate various dimensions of 'Britishness'; (3) its producers, directors and stars function both with and against Hollywood iconography and narrative forms; and (4) within the parameters of mass culture, it is possible to see 'how at any given moment a wide variety of discourses co-exist, each being representative of particular contemporary fears and anxieties which can be seen to operate at textual and subtextual levels' (p. 40). Thus competing discourses operate within all aspects of British cinema, calling attention to the shifting character of national boundaries.

In the final two chapters, Street turns to the overtly 'unofficial' British cinema exemplified by 'cinematic modernism', its tendencies to explore and valorize 'the visual rather than the verbal', 'interrogate linear modes of narration', 'explore psychological traits and abandon traditional forms of characterisation' (p. 147). Among the films she examines are those produced in the interwar period by the avant-garde of the documentary film movement, which include the political and the aesthetic avant-garde influenced by German expressionism and Soviet cinematic experimentation, the role of workers' film societies, and later in the 1940s to the 1970s the works of such feature film-makers as Alfred Hitchcock, Michael Powell and Emeric Pressburger, Joseph Losey and Nicholas Roeg. In more recent years (from 1966 to 1980) and especially identified with the London Filmmakers Co-Op and with the New American Cinema, film-makers pursued modernist political objectives through devices which sought to urge 'the spectator to take an active role in making meaning from images' (p. 170). Among the film-makers identified with 'structuralism', Street mentions Stephen Dwoskin, Laura Mulvey and Peter Wollen. In her analysis of 'counter-cultural' cinema in the 1980s and 1990s, Street focuses on the work of Peter Greenaway, Sally Potter, Derek Jarman, Terence Davies and Bill Douglas, as well as on black British and gay and lesbian film-making.

In the best sense of eclecticism, Street's volume has provided a wide range of perspectives from which to assess the nature and impact of cinema within British culture, offering a dazzling overview of the many and conflicting elements that constitute this 'national' cinema. The volume has balanced historical overview with nuanced and careful discussions of exemplary texts, events and individuals. Regrettably, in comparison to the discussion of earlier forms of film-making, the final section of *British National Cinema* focuses, perhaps too briefly and schematically, on contemporary black British film, on animation, and on gay and lesbian film-making. Furthermore, while the book acknowledges the important role that 'global, televisual networks' have played in the shattering of 'long-held notions of what is cinema, let alone what is British national cinema' (p. 3), *British National Cinema* does not pursue the implications of this observation, devoting its attention exclusively to cinema. Nevertheless, Street's book is an important, well-researched and balanced study of British cinema.

Brian McFarlane

UNITY, DIVERSITY AND DIAGNOSIS

Tom O'Regan, *Australian National Cinema* (London and New York: Routledge, 1996) 403 pp., ISBN 0-415-05730-2 £45.00 Hbk; ISBN 0-415-05731-0 £14.99 Pbk.

A 'hybrid form' and a 'messy affair' are two of Tom O'Regan's early characterizations of Australian cinema in this exhaustive and – it must be said at the outset – exhausting study of a national industry that has won its share of international notice in the past quarter century. The book's agenda is to elucidate the 'hybrid' and 'messy' aspects of Australian cinema, especially, but not wholly, in the period from the 1970s revival.

The book is organized into three parts: 'Making a national cinema', 'Making a distinct cinema' and 'Problematizing Australian cinema', each of which is divided into chapters and subdivisions, the headings for which, pedestrian as they often are, provide a key to the arguments. The aim is to provide a study of national cinema as a cultural phenomenon, with particular reference to placing Australian cinema in a theoretical framework which allows diagnosis of how it functions in the broader culture – cinematic and social – of which it is a manifestation and to which it contributes.

The idea of a national cinema is explored in relation to the dominance of Hollywood. This latter enjoins on the national a quest for difference *and* acceptance of a necessary degree of influence and similarity in terms of both product and market requirements. A national cinema, particularly an English-speaking one, will inevitably be constructed in the shadow of Hollywood, and it will often seem to be pitching its products somewhere between the mainstream, where Hollywood has the game sewn up, and art house and festival audiences. It will have both local and international affiliations of the most complex kinds, and O'Regan's painstaking research seems to have left no possibility unexplored.

His project involves discussion of ways in which Australian cinema is '*naturalized*' as a 'quasi-object' (e.g. through government support), '*socialized*', in the way that it charts existing social divisions and identities, and, I fear, '*discursivized*' through a series of often conflicting discourses, and '*problematized*' 'in the armoury of criticism' and as 'a technique of policy and governmental processes' (p. 36). He considers Australian cinema as a local and international forum, noting that Australian films recall the British in their anti-Americanness but echo the US in their putting down of the British. These two connections – the American and the British – are rightly seen as the major influential factors in the shaping of Australian cinema, aesthetically and industrially, and as a viewing experience. However, the increasing sense of an Asian factor, and other local and vocal constituencies, such as Aboriginal, feminist and gay, are carefully documented as to the ways in which they make their agendas felt in the production output.

O'Regan is scrupulous in charting the impulses – social, cinephile, political – which underlie the national cinema variant that has evolved in Australia. It is not possible in a short review to argue the toss with him over this or that viewpoint, but, just as one finds the argument drifting into large assertions about what national cinemas must be like, one finds the balancing effect of a subtly made point about, say, the 'dissension over the repertoire' as to 'the appropriate focus and ends of film production' (p. 153). His own purpose is summed up as 'to understand the fields in which Australian cinema circulates and comes to mean' (p. 162), those 'fields' emerging as both cinema-specific and more broadly and diversely 'cultural'.

To this end he canvasses film-makers, critics and reviewers, policy-makers at various levels, arriving many dense pages later at this formulation: 'I believe the best approach is to adopt pluralist ethics which allows for a diversity of equally valid ends' (p. 354). This is unexceptionable, but it hardly seems enough after so much detailed discussion of the complexity of Australian cinema. The most interesting part of the book is the central section in which O'Regan argues that 'there is no one Australian feature cinema' (p. 168) and proceeds to demonstrate the kinds of diversity which lead to this view, examining, for instance, the range of genres, social programmes and markets, and the kinds of emphases privileged by assorted film-makers and critics. He has a vast amount of accumulated evidence, with which the reader is bombarded from all directions, but in the end, and for all the careful headings and sub-headings, the book fails to arrive at a clear stance about the nature of Australian cinema and about its place in the culture at large. Its sum is less than its often provocative parts.

Whatever the book's merits, prospective readers should be warned that it is the most clumsily written and jargon-laden volume to have come this reviewer's way for a long time. For examples, note page 285 where the word 'problematization' occurs five times in seven lines, or such excrescences as 'representativity' and 'operationalizes' or usages such as 'rivalrous' and 'incestual', or frequent failures of agreement between subject and verb, or the recurring failure of hyphenation in such constructions as 'Hollywood oriented', or the endemic lapses in punctuation, or the common syntactical breakdown of sentences beginning with 'Like' ('Like the new German cinema, the search for an audience. . .'). It is no pleasure to draw attention to such solecisms; I have had occasion in the past to be grateful for O'Regan's work on national cinema, and the present work offers some reasons for continued gratitude. It is not common now to see reviews which draw attention to stylistic matters; in extenuation, I must say that they are so disfiguring that I cannot recommend the book to any but the most ardent student of national cinema who doesn't care in what form the information comes to him. Personally, I'm awaiting The Editor's Cut.

Briankle G. Chang

HOMING POSTMODERN

Steven Shaviro, *Doom Patrols: A Theoretical Fiction About Postmodernism* (New York: Serpent's Tail, 1997) 198 pp., ISBN 0-85242-430-3 $16.00 Pbk.

Seventeen proper names – whose collective appearance undoubtedly betrays a certain imaginary construction – chart the plot line of this 'theoretical fiction of postmodernism'. 'These proper names', the author cautions us at the outset, 'are fictional, even when they ostensibly refer to actual individuals. For they are not identities, but singularities' (p. vii). Using these fictional singularities as starting points, Shaviro builds a story about the so-called postmodernity by decoding for us what he thinks these singularities signify, by revealing to us what he takes to be the real messages encrypted in these singularities. In the process, proper names are read as tell-tale signs of cultural shifts, and nominal identities are treated as symptoms of changes in the social body, yielding, as a result, something resembling a manual for decoding what might be called the 'quotidian hieroglyphics' of the late twentieth century.

The story begins with *Doom Patrols*, a DC superhero comic co-produced by the writer Grant Morrison and various illustrators including Richard Case. Moving on from there, but constantly referring back to several characters in the comic, the story unfolds to envelope a wide variety of themes that have recently become all the rage: hybridity, gene manipulation, informatics, sociobiology, virtual reality, transsexuality, cloning, etc. What makes Shaviro's discussion interesting and informative is that these themes, rather than licensing techno-utopian speculations of which there is no shortage today, are ever so slightly transformed – shall I say, mediated – in the very telling of the story by another set of themes: protean ideas embodied in some of the most sexy writers on today's cultural studies reading list: Deleuze and Guattari, Foucault, Agamben, de Sade, Klossowski, Blanchot, Bataille, McLuhan, Richard Dawkins, Edward Wilson, Donna Haraway, among others. The result is a text that not only records Shaviro's virtual meetings with various hyperreal beings as he MOOs and MUDs across the cyber space, but also documents his critical reflections on a newly constituted dimension of today's digitally networked *Lebenswelt*, a dimension in which manufactured encounters between 'a brain in a vat' (Thomas Nagle) and *musca domestica* (Cronenberg's *The Fly*), between an insomniac Descartes and an even more insomniac Beckett, etc., are no longer fantastic narrative inventions but rather lived possibilities.

One of the factors that make Shaviro's reflections both convincing and incredible is the quasi-Hegelian perspective he brings to bear on the phenomena he analyses. Assuming a gaze similar to that which enables Hegel to see the 'spirit' reflected in 'a bone', Shaviro, too, detects the ascendance of postmodernity as an immanent reversal of certain local and ultra-mundane activities that take place in the interstices of our everyday lives. Thanks to his analyses, buttressed effectively with abundant personal testimonies, we learn to distinguish proper postmodern moments from those that history will actively forget. More importantly, we learn that most of our everyday practices, ranging from eating, drinking, cruising, having sex, to vacationing in Mundo Maya, are 'badly in need of replacement by newer and more high-tech models. It's simply a question of engineering – or of "imagineering", as the Disney corporation likes to put it' (p. 22). To readers even vaguely familiar with Shaviro's intellectual sources, the conclusion he draws should not be surprising: we have no choice but to 'push further and further, into ever new landscapes of simulation and delusion . . . to remake ourselves over and over again, frenetically chasing fashion, keeping up with state-of-the-art technology, and always being sure to purchase (or steal) the latest upgrades' (p. 22).

While it is refreshing to be told that seemingly frivolous bodily adventures are in reality deadly serious spiritual acts, or that the cause of one's angst is no different from the source of one's indescribable pleasure, the kind of Baudrillardean, pataphysical inversion of being and its *semblables* celebrated by Shaviro leaves much else to be desired. At the very least, it glides over many of the theoretical intricacies his analysis clearly demands. Let me give one example. Speaking of the absolute power of 'image' in shaping one's identity, thus explaining, not disingenuously, why a young girl 'must spend hours in front of the mirror, agonizing over the outfit for tonight's date', Shaviro concludes that 'the image precedes the object, reflection always has to come first' (p. 159). Clearly, Shaviro is trying to out-Lacan Lacan himself. But given the broader theoretical context in which the statement seeks to intervene, it is simply false to say that the image precedes the object and reflection comes first. For if there were no prior object to anchor the image, if there were no distinction between an object and its reflection, one would not be able to recognize the reflection in a mirror *as* a reflection, let alone identify oneself with the reflection as a desired or undesired image of oneself. That is to say, unless one knows beforehand what an original image looks like and knows the difference between what is and what is not a reflection of it, one would not even be able to *see* the reflection in the mirror as an image, still less as one's own. Moreover, even if we live in a world of pure simulation, a world completely void of material referents, we still need to have a sense, however vague, of the difference between an image and that which the image reflects, in order to maintain our existential consistency. Without this minimal awareness, the very meaning of 'having an image' will be lost, and it would not make sense to speak of reflection as either earlier or later than anything else. Shaviro's aversion to Lacan seems premature.

For Shaviro, postmodernism is more than a theoretical option or a stylistic choice; it is, as he says at several points in the book, the very air we breathe. While it is true that a postmodern *Geist* has permeated our atmosphere, it is equally true that the air one inhales comes from a space no more than three feet away from one's nose. And the air quality, as most of us are well aware, varies dramatically from place to place, even within one postmodern city block. *Doom Patrols* covers a sizeable surface of the world in which Shaviro and most of his likely readers live, and Shaviro digs deep to uncover the distinguishing features of a space-time to which he (and his readers) will gleefully attach the adjective postmodern. At the same time, not being able to inhabit Shaviro's body and live what it experiences, I cannot help feeling that much of what Shaviro sees on his patrol is for his eyes only. If every postmodern man is a singularity without identity, if, as Shaviro suggests, 'he is a perpetual becoming, an ungrounded projection into unknowable futurity' (p. 113), I, for one, would have a hard time imagining what a world populated by such metamorphically fluid Nietzscheans would look like, and, in that case, I doubt if we will ever be certain whether two individuals can ever come to inhabit a common world. The postmodern world according to Shaviro is a truly fascinating one, so fascinating that I am not sure if it overlaps with the one in which I myself eat, drink and grow old. For this reason, I can only conclude by repeating what Shaviro says at the beginning: 'This book is autobiographical, every word'.

Lola Young

LOOKING EAST

Matthew Bernstein and Gaylyn Studlar (eds), *Visions of the East: Orientalism in Film* (London and New York: I. B. Taurus, 1997) 330 pp., ISBN 1-86064-304-3 Hbk; ISBN 1-86064-305-1 Pbk. £14.95.

With Mira Nair's film *Karma Sutra* about to be released, a new version of *Madame Butterfly* already in the cinemas and the avowed Buddhist affiliations of the rich and famous – particularly film stars, of which Richard Gere and Sandra Bullock are but two examples – the West's cinematic fascination with Eastern otherness is still clearly in evidence. Bernstein and Studlar have brought together a collection of essays which make apparent some of the strengths and weaknesses of using the concept of Orientalism to analyse mainly earlier instances of European and North American films which explore the peoples and the terrain of these imaginatively constructed other worlds.

Of necessity, the essays in this volume refer repeatedly to Said's Orientalism: a number of them also engage with Ella Shohat's essay – the first in the collection – and Bernstein suggests that these two texts are the key coordinates for mapping the terrain of Orientalist cinematic discourse. Shohat's detailed examination of the gendering of colonial constructions is a very useful analysis of the various structural similarities between the representation of a range of other cultures.

In his Introduction, Bernstein refers to Michael Rogin's observation regarding the pivotal position occupied by African-Americans at certain key moments in North American film history and makes similar claims for films which have made use of North African or Asian themes. Although the weight given to *Casablanca*, for example, on account of the film's action taking place in North Africa, is contestable in terms of its representing a 'transformative cinematic moment', the point being made is useful for drawing attention to the sometimes tense, often contradictory relationship between cinema and its conceptualization of the Orient.

Of course, since Said's seminal text on Orientalist discourse, scholars are aware that the notion of the Orient is a discursive construction so powerful that for Western film-makers and cinema audiences, the resultant images are often perceived to be 'reality'. What, then, can we hope for all those children (and adults for that matter) who have seen the Disney version of *Aladdin* and enjoyed Robin Williams's self-indulgent, virtuoso voicing of the genie, whose characterization, according to Alan Nadel's argument, may be read as nuclear power – seen as an evil but beneficial power source – now in the possession of the despotic demonized leaders of the Orient in Iraq and Iran? This highlights an issue briefly raised by Bernstein in his Introduction but not really explained elsewhere, which is: What is this work for and where is it going? Something that was lacking for me was a clear case being made for the importance of some of the texts being studied. What is it that is so compelling about Disney's *Aladdin* and its implications that we need to expend so much intellectual energy on it? Attention to that issue raises the lack of information regarding ways in which audiences rework the material they see: the audience in terms of actual bodies is something to which references are made but never really dealt with fully.

There is much in this collection that is both interesting and provocative. Both Marina Heung and Adrienne L. McLean try to unpack and then reintegrate the conflicting, contradictory elements of sexuality, gender and ethnicity, although in McLean's essay there is a tendency to assume that ethnicity is an attribute of 'non-white' peoples. Of the different accounts about the Jean Gabin vehicle, *Pepe Le Moko*, Janice Morgan has most to offer in terms of a cogent and complex analysis of the intersections of various aspects of social identity. Antonia Lant's contribution links a general 'Egyptomania' – especially in the early decades of the twentieth century – with the development of the cinema and ways of speaking about that development. She points to a number of allusions to 'mummies', tombs and treasures in the language of critics and designers which suggests an interconnection between the fabric and trappings of cinema and a variety of colonialist tropes.

The broad interpretation of what was/is classified as the Orient constitutes a problem, and even though Said's work was rather more focused, the blurring around the edges inherent in the term as a result of the lack of clarity evidenced in Western fantasies induces a kind of neo-Orientalism at work here. There is a sense in which Orientalism is being reinscribed through its reiteration as a viable category, one whose precepts change little over time and from country to country. There is a related question about the amount of context necessary in order to allow the reader to be able to place a film: what might be the relevant social, cultural and political predicates implicated in the flourishing or diminishing of Orientalist discourse at any specific moment and in a particular location? These are problems for those of us attempting to do analytical work on issues of 'race', ethnicity and culture: how to describe and analyse without reinforcing the hegemonic power of these discourses. However, this text presents the interested student of Orientalism with a focused collection of writings which, although not offering any radical new insights into the field, does contribute to the overall understanding of how the trope of 'the Oriental' functions in a variety of film genres.

Notes on Contributors

Jane Blocker is Assistant Professor of art history at Georgia State University in Atlanta where she teaches courses on contemporary art, critical theory and performance. Her book *Where is Ana Mendieta? Identity, Performativity, and Exile* will shortly be published by Duke University Press.

Patrick Brantlinger is Professor of English at Indiana University. A former editor of *Victorian Studies*, he is the author of several books, including *Rule of Darkness: British Literature and Imperialism, 1830–1914*; *Fictions of State: Culture and Credit in Britain, 1694–1994*; and the forthcoming *The Reading Lesson: Mass Literacy as Threat in Nineteenth-Century British Fiction*.

Briankle G. Chang teaches cultural studies in the Department of Communication at the University of Massachusetts, Amherst. He is the author of *Deconstructing Communication: Subject, Representation, and Economies of Exchange* (University of Minnesota Press, 1996).

Judith Farquhar is associate professor of anthropology at the University of North Carolina, Chapel Hill. She has published extensively on cultural and epistemological issues in traditional medicine in modern China, and is currently working on a book project called 'Medicine's Body, Mao's Ghost: History and Habitus in Post-Socialist China.'

Marcia Landy is the author of British Genres: Cinema and Society 1930–1960 (Princeton University Press, 1991) and, more recently, Cinematic Uses of The Past (University of Minnesota Press, 1996). She teaches film studies at the University of Pittsburgh.

Brian McFarlane is an Associate Professor in the English Department of Monash University, Melbourne. His next book is *An Autobiography of British Cinema* (Methuen and BFI, 1997) and he is co-editing *The Oxford Companion to Australian Film*.

Tomoko Masuzawa teaches religious studies and cultural studies at the University of North Carolina, Chapel Hill. She is the author of *In Search of Dreamtime: Quest for the Origin of Religion* (1993). She is currently writing about the invention of 'world religions' and working on a book entitled *Victorians in Wonderland: the Discovery of 'Spirituality' in the Age of Dead Matter*.

Carol Mavor teaches art history and critical theory at the University of North Carolina, Chapel Hill. She is the author of *Pleasures Taken: Performances of Sexuality* *and Loss in Victorian Photographs*. She has just completed *Passionate Interiors: The Photographic Secrets of Clementina Hawarden, 1857–1864*, a book about the erotics of adolescence, sisterhood and the meeting of procreative and photographic reduplication.

Timothy Mitchell teaches politics at New York University where he is also Director of the Hagop Kevorkian Center for Near Eastern Studies. He is the author of *Colonising Egypt* and editor of a forthcoming collection of essays, *Questions of Modernity*, to be published by the University of Minnesota Press.

Aleks Sierz is theatre critic of *Tribune* and a cultural commentator whose work has appeared in many newspapers (e.g. the *Independent* and *New Statesman*) and academic journals (e.g. *Media, Culture and Society* and *New Theatre Quarterly*). He has an MA in arts criticism from City University, London.

Peter Stallybrass teaches English and comparative literature at the University of Pennsylvania. He is co-author with Allon White of *The Politics and Poetics of Transgression*, and *Language Machines: Technologies of Literary and Cultural Production*, which he co-edited with Jeff Masten and Nancy Vickers, is forthcoming from Routledge. With Ann Rosalind Jones, he has just completed *Worn Worlds*, a book about clothes and the formation of the subject in early modern England.

Lola Young is Professor of cultural studies at Middlesex University.

John W. Hartman Center for Sales, Advertising, and Marketing History Special Collections Library, Duke University

The J. Walter Thompson Research Grants Program

Three or more grants of up to $750 are available from the John W. Hartman Center for Sales, Advertising, and Marketing History, Special Collections Library, Duke University to: (1) graduate students in any academic field who wish to use the resources of the Center for research toward MA, Ph.D., or other postgraduate degrees; (2) faculty members working on research projects, or (3) independent scholars working on non-profit projects. Funds may be used to help defray costs of travel to Durham and local accommodations for researchers using any of the Hartman Center's collections; photocopies and other reproductions not included.

In addition to the regular Thompson grants described above, the Hartman Center will fund three J. Walter Thompson Research Fellowships. Each Fellow will receive a stipend of $1000 during their stay in Durham. Fellowships are available to researchers planning to spend a minimum of two weeks at Duke doing research that focuses on the J. Walter Thompson Company Archives.

The major collections available at the Hartman Center at the current time are the extensive Archives of the J. Walter Thompson Company (JWT), the oldest advertising agency in the US and a major international agency since the 1920s; the advertisements (1932+) and a moderate amount of agency documentation from D'Arcy, Masius, Benton & Bowles (DMB&B); and the Outdoor Advertising Association of America (OAAA) archives and related collections documenting billboard history. The Center holds several other smaller collections relating to nineteenth- and twentieth-century advertising and marketing, supported by a growing number of books, periodicals, films, and videos.

For more information about the Hartman Center Collections, visit our WWW site at http://scriptorium.lib.duke.edu/hartman/

Requirements: The next cycle of awards will be for use between December 1997 and December 1998. Request application information at any time; forms will be sent out beginning in summer 1997. Graduate student applicants: (1) must be currently enrolled in a postgraduate programme in any academic department, and (2) must enclose a letter of recommendation from the student's adviser or project director. Faculty and independent scholars must enclose a curriculum vitae. Please address questions and requests for application forms to: Russell S. Koonts, John W. Hartman Center for Sales, Advertising and Marketing History, Special Collections Library, Duke University, Box 90185, Durham, NC 27708–0185; Phone: 919–660–5833; Fax: 919–660–5934; e-mail: rkoonts@duke.edu

Deadlines: Applications for 1997–8 awards must be received or postmarked by 31 October 1997. Awards will be announced in December.